FRANKLY
KELLIE

FRANKLY KELLIE

BECOMING A WOMAN IN A MAN'S WORLD

KELLIE MALONEY

BLINK

bringing you closer

Published by Blink Publishing
107-109 The Plaza,
535 King's Road,
Chelsea Harbour,
London, SW10 0SZ

www.blinkpublishing.co.uk

facebook.com/blinkpublishing
twitter.com/blinkpublishing

Hardback: 978-1-910536-23-0
Paperback: 978-1-910536-50-6

A CIP catalogue of this book is available from the British Library.

Design by Blink Publishing

Printed and bound by Clays Ltd, St Ives Plc

1 3 5 7 9 10 8 6 4 2

Text copyright © 2015 Kellie Maloney Event and PR Management Limited;
and Kevin Brennan
All images © Kellie Maloney

Papers used by Blink Publishing are natural, recyclable products made from wood grown in sustainable forests. The manufacturing processes conform to the environmental regulations of the country of origin.

Every reasonable effort has been made to trace copyright holders of material reproduced in this book, but if any have been inadvertently overlooked the publishers would be glad to hear from them.

Blink Publishing is an imprint of the Bonnier Publishing Group
www.bonnierpublishing.co.uk

To Mum, Tracey, Emma, Sophie, Libby,
Rich, Robyn, Ollie, Jake, and my late father.
And to Winnie and Louie.

Acknowledgements

Special thanks to Linda Lawrie, my counsellor, Jan Upfold, Heather Ashton and all at TG Pals for their support; thanks also to Neil Sibley, Guy and Hazel Williamson, Joe Dunbar, Tommy and Donna Pratt and their family, Ray Hawkins, Tony Fry, Moya, my dear, late friend Rosalind who was there for me through some difficult periods, and to a couple of very special people, Kayleigh and Aaron. Thanks to Rebecca (Becks), the bossy Erica, Jamie from Portugal, my nephews Eugene and Tommy for their support and understanding, Mark and Sue Cole, Dee Kelly, Lauren Goodger, Edele Lynch, Audley Harrison, George Gilby, Ricci Guarnaccio and all the housemates; to Karen Jackson, Tommy Gilmour, Millwall Football Club and their fans for being so understanding and for their tremendous support, and to my aunts and uncles for the support they have given to my mum and me.

I would also like to thank John and Matt Hayes, Victoria and Amelia and all at Champions; the *Sunday Mirror* for the sympathetic way in which they handled such a sensitive issue; and to all the staff at Nuffield hospital in Brighton, in particular to Liz Hills, Andrew Yelland, Phil Thomas and Duncan Macdonald.

Thanks to my agent Tim Bates at Pollinger; to Clare Tillyer, Karen Browning, Joel Simons and everyone at Blink for their support and belief in this book, to all those who continue to follow me on Twitter @kelliefmaloney, and to many others who have shown their support along the way.

Finally, my thanks to Kevin Brennan, who has been a friend for more than 30 years, and who collaborated with me in writing this book, to his wife Lynda and their children, James and Rachel.

Contents

CHAPTER ONE

Calm before the storm

It had been a very strange week and my emotions were all over the place. Not surprising really, because I knew that in a matter of hours my secret would be out and the world would know I was a transsexual.

I sat in a small chalet at a holiday complex in Ilfracombe, Devon, going over everything. I'd gone there with a friend from my support group not really knowing what to expect. The one thing I was sure about was that at last I would be able to come out of hiding and be the person I was meant to be. How that person was going to be received by other people was a different matter. I was going into the unknown and I was petrified.

It was early in August 2014, and I'd spent time preparing for the moment and trying to get my head around exactly what was going to happen. The story of my lifelong inner conflict was going to be made public and splashed across the front page of a Sunday newspaper. It had been my decision to go public. I knew the chances of keeping my secret were getting slimmer and this was my way of trying to manage it. It all seemed very sensible when I made the decision and deep down I knew I was doing the right thing, but the closer I got to the story being out there, the worse I felt.

I had moments of calm as I tried to convince myself that all the stress and aggravation of living with my transgender issues would be made much easier. I would begin to feel relaxed but then the darker thoughts would start to invade my head as I imagined my life falling apart with the coming revelations. It was the uncertainty of it all that really began to worry me and the main concern was the effect it was going to have on my family. They had all been really supportive but I knew it had been difficult for all of them to come to terms with what was going on. Now they were going to have to face the fallout once the story broke in the media.

I had no real idea how it would go. I probably hoped for the best but expected the worst.

I knew I might have to put up with all sorts of idiots making comments and abusing me for what I was. What I didn't like the thought of was the backlash my family might suffer. It was not their fault – they were still coming to terms with the fact that someone they had known as a man all their lives now wanted to be a woman.

I'd been able to keep things hidden for so long by lying, deceiving and living a double life. As Frank Maloney I had made my life in boxing as the tough-talking, wise-cracking, cockney promoter and manager. I came from a macho working-class background and I managed Lennox Lewis when he was heavyweight champion of the world. I was a man's man, someone who wouldn't take any nonsense and who was always up for a night out with the boys. Some people liked me and some people hated me – it was par for the course as one of the major players in boxing. I didn't set out to upset people but it didn't bother me and it was all part of the package that was the public face of Frank Maloney.

But behind the public face another person had always lurked: Kellie, the woman I always wanted to be. In fact, it wasn't just a case of her being the woman I always wanted to be, it was more a case of Kellie being the real me. The truth was I had always been a woman trapped inside the body of a man, but in order to protect and hide that truth I had lived a lie all my life. It was easier to do that than to come clean with myself, my family, friends and the general public. Whether consciously or subconsciously, I used my image to hide behind. I constructed a barrier in order to keep my secret safe because I was convinced the boxing world would never come to terms with a transsexual as part of the sport. I believed it would have meant everything I'd worked for would have been destroyed. In a few months time I intended to have an operation which would enable me to fully transition from being a male to being a female. I would no longer have the body of a man, I would be a woman.

It had been easier to keep the secret earlier in my life but the urge to stop battling with my true feelings became more powerful as I grew older. There was no stopping the inevitable and in many ways I'd grown tired of trying to cover up the person I really was. I tried to maintain the two lives I was leading but it was impossible. I couldn't go on any longer. I had to be true to myself and to those closest to me or face the possibility of ending up in a coffin. In fact, in 2012 I'd already tried to take my life and the constant mood swings coupled with periods of depression would have taken me down that route once again.

So, after years of making headlines to promote my fights and boxers, I had announced my retirement from the sport and quietly slipped away from the business. I lived a private life for over a year before sitting down with a journalist from the *Sunday Mirror* newspaper to tell the story of my transgender issues. Once I'd made the decision to speak out, I had a sense of relief. I believed that what had often been a nightmare 12 months for me was finally going to be over. Whatever the reaction was going to be, at least I wouldn't have to go around looking over my shoulder all the time.

I was also looking forward to finally being able to discard Frank Maloney. For the last year I had lived something like 90 per cent of my life dressed as a woman, but because of the circumstances of my life at that time, I still had to be Frank on occasions. I had to dress as him if I was meeting certain people who knew nothing about the real me and I began to hate doing it. I began to resent the fact that I still had to dress as a man and that Frank was still around.

I would have days where I would travel to London from Kent and be dressed fully as a woman. Nobody batted an eyelid. I didn't get strange looks and I was fully accepted whenever I was in Kellie mode. Those days made me feel happy and confident. I was relaxed and pleased that I was able to be the real me, but when I had to return to being Frank I hated the pretence. Sometimes I hated myself for still trying to live a double life. The truth was it was necessary and I just had to put up with it until the article came out.

I knew there would be tough times ahead and I would turn the thing over in my mind, often lying in bed with tears streaming down my face as the darker thoughts began to take over. There were so many nights when I went to bed hoping that I wouldn't wake up. So many people knew me as the confident and, at times, arrogant Frank but that certainly wasn't the case when I was alone in my bed at night. I felt vulnerable and afraid.

The brashness I displayed as Frank Maloney wasn't there as I lay awake as Kellie until the early hours of the morning.

I'd wake up at all sorts of times, often taking my two airedale dogs, Winnie and Louie, for long walks before dawn as I tried to get my head straight and pull myself out of depression. Those dogs really helped me. It may sound strange, but no matter how bleak I felt I knew I was responsible for them. I honestly believe the bond I have with them helped me through some pretty bad moments when no other human being was around. They saw me at my worst and they sensed just how upset and emotional I was at times.

Deep down I knew that there was no stopping the process I'd set in motion. I was going to be a woman and put right what had been wrong at birth. I was going to fully transition and be honest with myself. I knew that the only way I could really hope to have any chance of living a normal life and being happy was to be honest with the public as well. I had courted publicity in my working life and that was part and parcel of being a boxing promoter. I had to sell the shows I was staging and put bums on seats. My business was also to get publicity for the boxers I managed, raising their profiles and enhancing their careers in the process. I became famous as a by-product – managing Lennox Lewis sent my public profile through the roof. I enjoyed it and benefitted from it financially but it also meant that when my transgender issue began to gather pace, I had some big decisions to make.

Ideally, I would have loved to have just disappeared. It was something I'd dreamed of doing, but in the end I wasn't able to and so I'd had to make a decision about exactly what I was going to do. Using the *Sunday Mirror* in order to come out and tell my story was something I agonised over for a long time, but once the decision had been made there was no turning back.

I wasn't sure what would happen when the paper appeared, but I knew that I didn't want to be at home in Maidstone. I took myself off to Ilfracombe to weather the storm that I was convinced would follow publication. I set off with my friend Roz to the West Country, feeling nervous.

I'd already seen the copy and the *Mirror* had kept to their word and written what I considered to be a positive piece. So often in the past I'd read stories about people in the transgender community that angered and upset me. They often seemed to poke fun at the individuals concerned when being a transsexual and wanting to transition is not a trivial matter. People who do it often have to go through hell in order to be the person they really ought to be.

It was a long journey, but it was nice to have someone with me. There was lots of small talk and a few laughs as we drove, but there was no getting away from the nagging thought at the back of my head, what would things be like tomorrow when the story was out and everyone knew?

Along the way I got a call from Alan Hubbard, a sports journalist with *The Independent* who I'd known for years. We hadn't spoken for a while, but he was a nice guy and knew his boxing. Alan laughed and sounded a bit awkward as he finally came to the reason he'd phoned me. 'Frank,' he said, 'look, there's a story doing the rounds that the *Sunday Mirror* are going to print something about you having a sex change.'

I couldn't believe it. There had been so much planning gone into trying to maintain secrecy. The *Mirror* was even going to use a completely different story in their first edition which was distributed in the early hours of the morning making sure my story was held back for their final edition so that none of their rivals would have a chance to react to it and now here was Alan telling me he'd heard what was to come. Of course, I denied it.

'Don't be stupid,' I told him, 'Alan, I can't help what people might be saying, but there's no truth in it.'

I told him I was actually on holiday and our brief chat seemed to satisfy his curiosity. He probably thought the rumour was so outlandish that he was happy to take my word for it. I couldn't help smiling to myself after the call, thinking how throughout our conversation I had been dressed as a woman, in full Kellie mode! I later found out that there were rumours floating around throughout the day.

Ilfracombe wasn't exactly what I expected. The chalet was basic which was fine, and all the other people there were busy with their own summer holidays, which meant they were never likely to pay me any attention. One thought that did panic me a little was the possibility that I might be recognised the next day when my face would be all over the newspaper, but I comforted myself with the thought that all the pictures that were due to appear had me in a dark wig. I was now dressed as a blonde and I also made sure that I had a few pairs of big sunglasses that covered a large part of my upper face.

Once we arrived it was a case of making ourselves as comfortable as possible and then the long wait began. Of all the thoughts that were racing through my head that night, the one that kept coming back to me was that the only people who really mattered were my family and I knew I had their support. If it was going to be us against the world then I knew they were going to be there for me and I always wanted to be there for them. That thought gave me a lot of strength and as the night wore on I became a bit more relaxed about the situation.

I was sent copies of the pages that would appear the next day and for the first time I was able to see what it would look like. I'd already seen the words, but seeing the actual pages with the pictures was a very different experience and the realisation of what was about to happen hit home.

This thing was going to happen. My story would soon become public knowledge and in a strange way the inevitability of it all helped me to relax. Ever since I was a kid I knew there was something different going on inside me. As time went on I became very adept at concealing who and what I really was. In just a few hours all of that would stop. Frank would disappear for ever and Kellie would be able to be the woman she always wanted to be.

CHAPTER TWO

Dream girl

I felt really happy as we all played together. The other kids were my friends and it was nice joining in the games and having fun. We weren't doing anything special, just having a good time and laughing a lot over silly things. The sky was blue, the sun was out and the girls looked nice in their dresses. It felt good to be with them, I was happy and contented and then it happened as it always did. I woke up. I was no longer the happy, carefree little girl I'd been in my dream. Instead, I was Francis Maloney, a little boy who'd just had another one of his dreams. The dreams weren't always the same, but the theme was a recurring one. When I dreamed, I was always a little girl and not a little boy.

I was probably no more than four or five years old at the time and I found it very confusing. I didn't have dreams every night, but when I did they always seemed to involve me being a girl. I never had dreams about playing football or doing all the male things you might think of being a boy growing up in south London. In fact, I never had any sort of dream where I was a boy.

At that age I don't think I was old enough or mature enough to start analysing what was happening while I was asleep, but it was puzzling. I do remember wondering why I saw myself as a girl in the dreams and I did feel distinctly uncomfortable about the whole thing but I didn't think too deeply about it. They happened, I woke up and then I would get on with my young life as best I could. In a strange way I think I just began to accept them. They became part of life.

I was born in 1953 at Lambeth hospital in south London. My parents were both Irish. Mum Maureen was from County Wicklow and my father, Thomas, came from Roscrea in County Tipperary. I was the oldest of three boys. Eugene came along three years after me and the youngest, Vince, was born 18 months after him. The environment I grew up in was very typically Irish working class and, because all my siblings were boys, I suppose it was also quite male-dominated. The trouble was, a lot of what was expected of me just didn't feel right. I knew I was not like my brothers and I also knew that I wasn't really like the other boys I played with. I got on well enough with all of them, but I can't say I enjoyed the rough and tumble.

My very early recollections of that time are of me being more interested in girls than boys. I didn't actually play with them, but I would always look at the way they dressed and try to listen to their conversations. I had a fascination with them and the way they acted. I think now that it was as if I was trying to learn from them. To see the way they went about their lives and what they got up to. I suspect I often stared at them as well but it wouldn't have been seen as anything out of the ordinary at the time. I think I was probably laying the foundations for a pattern of behaviour that would help protect and hide my real feelings for many years to come. I may have done a lot of it subconsciously, but even when you're very young you instinctively pick up on things. I didn't want to be seen as different and so I blended in.

To a large extent it worked for me and like any other kids at the time there was plenty of things going on in the streets to occupy me. There were always games being played and I didn't really have time to sit and think, and I didn't have to confront the fact that there seemed to be something different about me. But when the dreams filled my head as I slept at night, they always left me with unanswered questions about why I had them and how I always saw myself as a little girl.

I started to think about them and wonder what they meant as I got older. They weren't horrible dreams. In fact, I always felt really happy in them and nothing but nice things seemed to happen. In one dream I ended up getting married and in another I was at a party laughing and running around as we played games. But at the same time, when I woke up and realised I wasn't the happy young girl of my dreams, the whole experience took on a much darker feel and at times it was quite disturbing. Sometimes I would wake up in a cold sweat feeling drained.

I realised pretty quickly there was no way I could speak to my mum or dad about what was going on in my head at night. I knew it wasn't normal and I knew it happened far too often for it just to be a coincidence. It was a part of what I was and that was pretty scary for a young kid. Was I mad? Why would I dream I was a girl? What could I do about it? When would it stop? I didn't have answers to any of the questions, but other things happened when I was awake to make me realise I really wasn't like the other boys.

I would often look at myself in the mirror and not really like what was staring back at me. All I could see was a little boy, standing in his shirt and shorts, but what I wanted to see was a pretty little girl dressed up nicely like the girls in my dreams. It was incredibly difficult to come to terms with and I obviously didn't have the maturity or knowledge to deal with the situation. I think that I slowly began to feel as though I was in some way trapped in the wrong body. The nagging feeling of being different from other boys was never very far away. It was an effort to play cops and robbers, run-outs or pretend to be soldiers, but I didn't want to be left out.

When I was quite young I actually used to hang around with a girl called Linda, who was the daughter of our landlord. She was a bit older than me but I felt comfortable with her. I used to like watching the way she acted and seeing the toys she played with. I felt at ease with her and very happy. She was kind and gentle which I instinctively liked. That relaxed and carefree feeling was never really there when I was playing with the boys.

I also remember when I was quite young becoming friends with a little boy who was black. Back then you didn't really see too many black kids around where I lived and it must have been quite difficult for him at times. I liked him and we got on well. I think part of the reason for befriending him was the fact that somewhere in my young mind I instinctively saw him as being like myself. We were both outsiders.

I was quite shy when I was young and certainly not the confident, outspoken person I became in boxing. The one thing that I did instinctively like was sport and my love of football started at a really young age. My dad took me to my first match at Millwall, where I watched the game sitting on a wall at The Den. I was only three years old but I loved being taken by my dad and, even now, the club is still an important part of my life.

I was well aware of the role I was supposed to play in my family. As the oldest of three brothers my dad had a very clear idea of what I should do and not do as a kid, and also of what I should aim to be as an adult. It was very much about working hard to make sure I got a good job and then it was about getting married, having children and providing for my own family. There was nothing odd in that as far as my father was concerned. He just wanted the best for his sons and tried to instil in me the sort of work ethic that actually did help me in later life.

Because my dreams were unsettling if I thought about them too much, I tried not to pay them much attention. I didn't want to be seen as different by anyone. I just wanted to be the same as all the other boys. Except that deep down I knew I wasn't and probably never would be.

CHAPTER THREE

Relative values

I think I was probably closer to my mum than I was to my dad when I was a young boy. I loved both of them, but I always felt more comfortable with my mum and wanted to be with her. My dad was quite an intimidating figure and even as a kid I could see that there were clearly defined roles in our household when it came to the man and the woman. They were both really hard-working. He was employed by British Rail doing construction and she had a job as a waitress and, like so many other women, mum was the glue that kept the family functioning.

Dad liked a drink and a bet but it never interfered with his work and he always used to tell me that you made sure you turned up for work, no matter what. He had very definite ideas about what men and women should do when it came to the family. If I ever tried to help my mother around the house he would very quickly tell me to stop and say that things like cleaning and tidying up was women's work. He didn't even think I should help my mum with carrying bags when she went shopping. He wasn't a bully or a violent man, he was just very set in his ways. He always liked to have his dinner on the table when he came home from work and it always seemed to be meat and two veg no matter what.

He loved all of his sons and was always there to try and help in the best way he could, but I can't honestly say he was the sort of dad who would put me on his knee and give me a cuddle. That just wasn't him. But I think he knew he'd made some mistakes in his life, as we all do, and he didn't want his kids to do the same. I'm sure he would have loved us to have stayed on at school and maybe go to university because he recognised that education could be the key to having a successful life and that was certainly what he wanted for all three of us.

I'd always be fascinated by watching my mum do everyday things and from very early on I think I got a sense of how she made things tick for the family. Apart from having her own job she seemed to do so much – shopping, cooking, cleaning, making sure we were all looked after. She never seemed to stop. She used to love dressing her three boys in the same style of jumpers – which she'd knit for us – and I remember enjoying helping her look after Eugene when he was a baby. I'd fetch bottles for her so she could feed him his milk.

I also recall feeling comforted by her clothes. I didn't dress up in them but I would sometimes hold them close to me and it made me feel calm. I'm sure it was more of a comfort thing. I had a couple of teddy bears when I was really young, but I actually felt I got more comfort from being able to hold some of my mum's clothing than I did from cuddling the bears or holding any of my other toys.

Our flat in Gipsy Hill, south London, was tiny and my mum and dad slept in the front room on a makeshift bed. But we were happy and I remember having some lovely summer holidays back in Ireland, in Dublin and in the countryside of Tipperary, although they weren't exactly what you would call family holidays. We stayed with various members of the extended family, and mum and dad would sometimes come out with us but invariably one or other of them would have to return to London for work. It was never as if we spent that much time all together.

For a brief period I went to school in Ireland because we had to move out of our flat and there was nowhere for us to stay. School out there when I was seven was a pretty awful experience. The lessons were in Gaelic, which was obviously a nightmare for an English kid, but the worst aspect of the whole depressing episode was the group of sadistic nuns who ran the place. They walked around carrying huge sticks in their hands and lashed out at any poor kid who they thought might be doing something wrong. I was so relieved to finally leave the place and head back to the familiarity of south London.

We moved into a large Victorian house in Camberwell Green, just a few miles north of Gipsy Hill. The place had been converted into a couple of flats and ours was huge. Each of us had our own bedroom as well as the luxury and novelty of a family bathroom for the first time in my young life. I was sent to St Joseph's school nearby where again I did my best to fit in. I played sport and hung out with the boys, but there was still no denying the fascination I had for the girls. I would watch them playing together and think that I'd like to be joining in and playing with them. That feeling of being different was very much part of my thoughts. There was nothing I could put my finger on, no one thing that made me feel this way, it was just something inside me that was nagging away and saying, 'You're not like the other boys. You're different.'

We moved home again just before I was due to leave my primary school and go to Sacred Heart secondary school in Camberwell New Road. But we didn't move far and the new place was a large house owned by St James's church in Peckham. The downstairs area was the church's social club and it had a full-size snooker table. The basement area had table-tennis and there was a room big enough to play other sports such as badminton. The facilities made us popular with the boys in the area and we would take full advantage with our friends. As I genuinely liked sport I joined in with any game any time I could. This did me no harm at all in terms of fitting in with the other boys and, although I wasn't great at things like football, I was one of those kids who always put my heart and soul into playing a game. At school my choices were different. I took domestic science over woodwork.

My mum has since told me that she sensed I was different to my brothers and that when I was young she recalled that I often had periods where I seemed to be withdrawn. I honestly can't remember that, but it sounds right when I think about it now with all that I know about myself. I was clearly confused with how I felt and reacted in certain situations and the older I got the more aware I was of it. The dreams were still there, but I couldn't bring myself to talk about them and so I suspect I just kind of retreated into myself.

I had an aunt who was involved in the fashion business and she would often bring stuff over to store at our place. I remember once discovering a load of sequined dresses in a cupboard, along with really nice headgear for women. I secretly started trying them on and wearing them, making sure I carefully put them back in exactly the same place as I had found them. I was probably only about 11 or 12 at the time, and when I saw them I just couldn't help myself. You have to remember that I'd had a fascination with the way girls and women dressed and behaved since I was very young. I'd pictured myself as a little girl in all of those dreams. So when there was a chance to try on such glamorous women's clothes, I just couldn't resist the temptation. How did I feel? I couldn't honestly tell you. I think there was definitely a sense of excitement, but that might also have been due to the fact that I was desperate not to get caught. I just felt compelled to do it, as if there was something deep inside me driving me on to do it. I remember feeling happy, but then there was probably a sense of regret because there was something else inside me telling me that it was normal. But if it was normal, why would I be so afraid of being caught? I'm not sure if I felt ashamed that I'd done it and I think that once I'd put the clothes back I just got on with being the little Francis Maloney that everyone knew. What I do know is that having discovered the cupboard, the fascination with what was inside it was always lurking somewhere in my mind.

By this time I knew very clearly that being a boy didn't seem right to me. In my quiet moments I would cry, wishing that I could be a girl. I would go to bed at night in tears and when I went to church I sometimes prayed that I would somehow wake up the next morning as a girl. At the same time, I wanted to please my mum and dad. I knew that if I did try to talk about what I was going through, people would think that there was something wrong with me mentally. I think that about this time I became very much aware that I should strive to be the sort of son my dad wanted. I didn't want to let him down.

I struggled at school and was certainly not academic, but I now know that having dyslexia didn't exactly help my cause. I had problems reading and writing which often made life difficult for me, but in those days nobody really seemed to understand how kids could be affected by dyslexia and the way information on a page could appear confusing. It was just interpreted as a lack of intelligence. I can't blame it for the way I seemed to struggle with so many things at school, but having learnt more about the condition over the years, I know it didn't help. Having dyslexia was probably another reason for liking sport so much – I didn't have to read or understand things to play games, kick or throw a ball and run around. Then there was boxing.

I was 11 when I first put on a pair of boxing gloves, encouraged by our PE teacher, Mr Sally, who one day decided to organise a tournament at the school. I boxed a kid called Ray Callaghan who was bigger and stronger than me and there were a few laughs when I stepped into the ring but it really didn't bother me. I lost the bout on points and cried because I desperately wanted to win but I also realised that I liked the idea of boxing. I don't think it had anything to do with me trying to project a macho image – although it didn't do any harm on that front – but I was into it as an individual sport. I also really enjoyed the training. I was still pretty shy but I could lose myself in boxing and that appealed to me.

Two years later I was attracted to the idea of becoming a priest. Because of my Irish family background, the Catholic church had always been a big part of my life. My mum and dad weren't fanatical about religion, but it meant a lot to them and that feeling transferred to me. We had some missionaries who gave a talk to the school and their stories sparked something in my imagination – and perhaps the idea of joining the priesthood had something to do with my confused state of mind as an early teen. I'd been to Lourdes as an 11-year-old and the stories of miracles had a real effect on me. I had never lost my interest in religion. I was an altar boy at our church, St James's, taking part in weddings and funerals, so the church thing was always there in the background.

The idea of becoming a priest was encouraged by my headmaster, Mr Timmins, who later became a Christian Brother. It was also Mr Timmins who first called me Frank – until I joined the school I'd always been Francis. I liked Frank because it sounded tougher, like something out of an American gangster movie – although I don't remember too many American gangsters being dressed in shorts, something my mum continued to do until I was 13. I became deadly serious about the priesthood and my parents were probably proud that their son wanted to explore the possibility of becoming a priest, just like any good Irish Catholic mum and dad would be. I suspect they thought it would only be a five-minute wonder – and they weren't far wrong. Nevertheless, they were happy to go along with my plan to join the Mill Hill Missionaries and I spent time at a seminary in Freshfield, Liverpool. But after three weeks or so I realised the whole thing wasn't really for me. The reality of what you needed to do in order to become a priest was just too alien. I didn't have the dedication for it.

Maybe I was hoping that religion would solve my problem; that there would be some kind of miracle and my thoughts about being a girl would go away or that I would actually become a girl. To be truthful, I don't really know what I was thinking. I was genuinely inspired by the stories of the missionaries but the reality was not what I had bargained for. I was shown to a huge dormitory when I arrived at the seminary and told that was where I would be staying during my time. That was the first sign that the place wasn't right for me. I was also expected to stay silent and spend long hours studying the Bible, all of which just made me feel uncomfortable. So it was back to south London and the comfort of my familiar surroundings.

But I'd wanted to find out about the priesthood. I hadn't done it for a laugh or on a whim. I was serious. The more I've thought about it over the years, the more I believe the confusion I was suffering over my own identity might have had something to do with my decision to go up to Liverpool. The church might have offered me the mental comfort and reassurance I needed or perhaps the thought of becoming a priest offered me an escape from my confusion. I don't entirely know. But even when I was thinking of becoming a priest, I wondered what it would be like if I was a little girl and whether I would want to become a nun.

It is difficult for any teenager to come to terms with all sorts of things in their lives, including puberty. I was no different in that sense, but there was the added difficulty of trying to figure out exactly what was going on inside me. I looked like a boy and was expected to behave as one while my brain was telling me I was a girl. I wanted to know more about what was wrong with me and the way that I felt, but there simply wasn't any real information out there for a teenager – or if there was, I had no idea of where to find it. I realised there might be books on the subject, but there was no way I was ever go into my local library to find them. This was the mid-1960s and the world was becoming a very different place for young people, but as a 13-year-old in Peckham with gender identity problems from an Irish working-class background, I can't say I really felt part of the swinging '60s.

My male friends had all started to take an interest in the opposite sex. There was a girl at school called Margaret Dooley who used to leave me little notes on my desk saying how much she liked me. I don't think she realised it, but those notes did me a lot of good with my mates. They would pull my leg and joke that she fancied me but it helped to make me seem normal. I was seen as one of the lads. On the face of it, that's exactly what I was.

I went to watch Millwall, boxed and now there was a girl from school after me. All very normal and that's exactly how I wanted it. I wasn't deliberately covering up my dreams and feelings about wanting to be a girl but I really did want to be just like all the other boys. I thought that the more I acted in a normal way and did all the things that were expected of me, the more likely it was that all my other thoughts would start to go away. Doing masculine things could chase away those other thoughts and desires.

Physically, I was small for my age, but I can't honestly say I ever saw that as a problem and neither did any of the other boys. I started to box on a regular basis for the Dog Kennel Hill club – named after the road they were located on – known as the DKH. Being fit and active was good for me and my dad was pleased to see me getting into the sport. He loved the idea of his kids playing sport and I even had a trial with Wimbledon football club one snowy winter morning when they were still a non-league club. I was told by the guy in charge of the trial to come back some time later when I'd grown a bit bigger. I never went back and never really grew any bigger, because by that time I'd reached my adult height of 5 feet 3 inches.

Boxing became a big part of my life as I threw myself into it, competing at amateur level in the Feds (London Federation of Boys' Clubs Championships) and the Junior ABA (Amateur Boxing Association) Championships. I boxed at venues like the Hilton hotel in London's Park Lane and the Café Royal but I certainly didn't have the natural talent to be destined for the top. I soon realised that I wasn't going to be a world champion but I had determination and was always prepared to have a go whenever I stepped through the ropes. I still often felt uncomfortable with who I was and would have my familiar dreams, but to the outside world I had carved out a very normal life.

I knew that I was different to my brothers. The pair weren't that alike, but it was more that I instinctively felt that whatever was going on inside me set me apart. Eugene was three years younger than me but he seemed to grow up really quickly and was always getting into scrapes. Vince was quieter and more than four years younger than me. We were just all different as I'm sure brothers in other families are, but I felt I should have been their sister rather than their brother and yet I couldn't give any indication to anyone at home – or at school. We had someone in our class who was a little bit backward and he was picked on mercilessly. Kids can be horrible and if they find some kind of weakness they go for it in a big way. There were a couple of boys who some of the other kids thought might be gay or 'queer', as homosexuals were often called back then. There was no proof that they were. I just think they weren't the sort of boys to join in with the crowd and maybe didn't do the things expected of them. I didn't think I was gay but I just wasn't sure exactly what I was. I knew I didn't look at other boys and fancy them. There was no sexual attraction, but if I had dreams about being a girl and actually wished I was female, what did that make me?

In a strange sort of way, I think taking part in masculine activities helped to reassure me. In my own mind I was trying to be as normal as possible and in doing that I was able to feel that whatever was inside me was being beaten. The more normal I acted, the more normal I would become. I suppose I hoped it might be a phase I was going through, but when I was being honest with myself, I knew it wasn't some fad that I would grow out of. This was something that was part of me and I had to find ways of coping with it.

I suspect that both of my brothers knew I was a bit different. Eugene always used to call me 'Goody two-shoes' because I would never go that step further with things. He was always headstrong and a bit of a tearaway. He wasn't a kid for too long because he was getting up to all sorts of things as a young teenager and, despite him being younger, there never really seemed to be much of a gap between us. He was loud, confident and not afraid to push his luck. My dad loved all of his sons, but I can't help feeling that he had a bit of a soft spot for Eugene, even if my brother caused him and my mother some real headaches over the years. Because we were close in years we tended to do quite a bit together as he got into his late teens and early 20s, but even as a young kid he'd get up to all sorts of things, some of which were a bit dubious.

Eugene must have been the only 14-year-old kid in Peckham who was driving around in a gleaming white Bentley! It's absolutely true and to this day I really don't know where he got it from. My dad asked me one day if I knew anything about Eugene driving. I just started laughing because the notion seemed farfetched, but dad was adamant he was right because some of his pals had told him they'd actually seen Eugene, along with one of my brother's mates, Tony Hudson and some giggling girls in the back seat. I still wasn't convinced, but sure enough a few days later I saw a lovely white Bentley driven by my brother. Eugene gave me some story about how he and Tony had managed to buy it with the proceeds of some 'bits and pieces' they'd been up to.

Eugene and Tony were really good friends and they used to egg each other on. They were characters from a very young age and both were prepared to take risks to get what they wanted. Some years later the they got jobs working for a diamond merchant in London and had managed to fill their pockets full of stuff they shouldn't have had. They were delighted with their little scheme but then got a shock as they walked towards Holborn underground station and a policeman tapped them on the shoulder. They froze, thinking their luck had run out, only to find it was

Johnny Banham, a coach and trainer to the Metropolitan police team who had recognised the two of them because both Eugene and Tony boxed as amateurs. Johnny only wanted their help in an identity parade. They were relieved and happy to talk boxing with Johnny on the way to the police station. He even dropped them back at the underground when they'd finished and the two of them laughed all the way home with their pockets stuffed full of what they had 'acquired'.

But despite the kind of masculine image I was constructing for myself something inside me always enabled me to pull back and steer clear of things that might get me into real trouble. There were the odd scrapes and skirmishes, such as getting involved with the football hooligan culture of the late 1960s, but I was always on the periphery. Every club would have a group of fans who were prepared to fight with the opposition supporters, sometimes on the terraces at the ground or often in the streets surrounding it. They were very different times, but it was all part of what you did as a teenager and I joined in the things my friends got up to even when I felt naturally reluctant to be part of something. I just went along because it would have been very difficult for me to turn away and not do the things my mates were doing.

On one memorable occasion in the early hours of the morning when a group of us couldn't get a taxi, we nicked a bus! We took it from the local garage so that we could get home but not surprisingly got stopped by the police. Most of us got off with a warning as I don't think they could believe how cheeky we were to attempt a stunt like that. The guy who was driving wasn't so lucky – he was charged. I think they wanted to make an example of him.

My world back then was full of characters, whether in the football team I played for, at the boxing club or hanging around with my mates at school. The café in Peckham Rye railway station was also great place – you could go in there and be guaranteed to find someone who could get you whatever you wanted, from shoes to clothes, televisions and cars. There was always a guy who knew where he could 'lay his hands' on anything for you. I loved seeing these people in action. I also used to love going to the West End to shop. From very early on in my teens I developed a love for clothes and even though I still had thoughts of being a girl and dressing as one I knew I had to stick to male clothes in reality. At least fashion had changed in the 1960s and boys' clothes were no longer as boring – there was much more colour and far more variety.

Liking clothes was one thing but being able to afford them was often quite another. My mum and dad weren't poor but they certainly weren't rich. There was never really any feeling that spare cash was hanging around the place. It was all hard-earned money and it went on running the household and looking after my two brothers and me. I did various little jobs as a kid to earn a bit of cash for myself and I also joined in some of the scams my mates would get up to in order to get ourselves a bit extra. We'd nick lemonade bottles from crates at the back of shops and then go around to the front and take them back in because they would give you money back on the bottles. It was nice to have a bit of money in my pocket although things like that hardly gave me enough to go on a shopping spree. But in the spring of 1966 – when I was 13 – I really hit the jackpot.

I played for a football club managed by my dad and he'd won a couple of tickets to the FA Cup final between Everton and Sheffield Wednesday. He gave them to me so that I could go along to Wembley with my mate, Micky Griffin. The FA Cup final was probably a bigger deal back then. It was as if the whole country came to a halt for the afternoon. The tickets were always like gold dust and a lot of fans travelled to the game in hopes of buying one from a tout on the day.

Micky was desperate to see the game and we were both really excited about the prospect of being at the Cup Final, something we'd only ever seen on the television before. When we got there the place was buzzing with supporters from both clubs and it wasn't long before we were being asked if we had any tickets we wanted to sell. When I heard how much people were prepared to pay for the two we had, I did a quick re-think about just how much we wanted to see the game. I decided it was far better to take the cash for the tickets and I headed off to the West End for a bit of a shopping spree, but I made sure I met up with Micky later that day to find out the result of the game in case my dad asked what had happened.

I had struggled academically throughout my school days and I couldn't wait to take the first opportunity I got to leave. In those days you could do that at 15, which was a real relief, but then I had the problem of deciding exactly what I was going to do to earn a living. My dad had always drummed into me the importance of working hard and earning money. Once he realised I wasn't going to leave school with a stack of qualifications to my name, he wanted to make sure I went into something that was going to give me money and some degree of security. The sort of job that meant I might have to start at the bottom, but could work my way up the ladder and learn a trade at the same time.

My dad had always been interested in horse racing and loved to have a bet. It wasn't something that ever interested me, but he'd got to know a bookmaker from Rotherhithe called Eddie Reid who told him that that there was a stable in Epsom who were always looking for young lads to become apprentice jockeys. My dad thought my stature might be ideally suited and so I was sent off to Epsom Downs. I think he had become a little bit concerned by the fact that I seemed to be spending more times hanging around with my mates than I did looking for a job.

Being an apprentice jockey did appeal to me in some ways and I was certainly prepared to give it a go, but that very soon changed when the realities of the job became apparent. Believe me, trying to make it as a jockey was no easy business. Riding a horse was only a small part of what you were expected to do. It felt more like slave labour to me and after six weeks of trying to make it work, I'd had enough of the place. I found the whole thing demeaning and I couldn't wait to leave. I was treated so poorly and I couldn't understand how anyone could put up with it. The other apprentices were okay and I never really had a problem with them, but the daily regime was something I just wasn't cut out for.

After the unhappy experience in Epsom, my dad turned to a friend in the catering business who suggested it might be worth me trying my hand at being a chef. I got an interview and was then offered a job at a Ministry of Defence establishment near Shaftesbury Avenue in the West End. It was a good opportunity and it also gave me the chance to start studying at Westminster catering college for my City and Guilds certificates. I was really pleased to get the chance of such a decent job which offered prospects, but quickly began to think I'd made the wrong decision.

I was put off by the brain-numbing job of preparing 600 sausages but it was another encounter that almost ended my career in catering before it started. There was a guy there called Eric who seemed very friendly on my first day, helping me with my oversized uniform and making little jokes which I thought he was doing to help me settle in. But it wasn't very long before I realised there was another side to Eric's friendliness. As I was rolling the sausages, he came up behind me, put his hand on my backside and made some remark about what he would like to do to me. For a split second I think I froze, but then another instinct took over very quickly and I could feel anger building up. There was a knife on the table and I instinctively grabbed it and planted the blade into the back of the hand he was using to lean on the table. I'm amazed nobody heard his screams and I don't think he could believe what I'd just done, but the feeling was mutual: I couldn't quite believe what he'd obviously wanted to do to me. It was a really nasty experience and Eric very quickly realised that he'd picked on the wrong kid to try and have some fun with. I also told him where I'd stick the knife if he ever tried anything like it again and from then on Eric steered clear of me and allowed me to continue my apprenticeship in peace.

Despite my questions about my gender identity, I knew that I didn't fancy men. I'd gone over things in my head so many times and I had wondered at times if my feeling when it came to wanting to be female meant that perhaps I was gay but I was never sexually attracted to men. By this time I had more of an idea of exactly what my problem was. The trouble I had at this time was trying to find out more.

April Ashley had been outed by the *Sunday People* as a transsexual in 1961 and was the first Britain to undergo sex-change surgery and to have fully transitioned. At the time the story came out I was only eight and the whole thing passed me by but as I'd got older I'd caught other references to her in newspapers. They said she had been born a boy but knew that she should have been born a girl. I found the whole thing fascinating and wanted to know as much as I could about her and what had gone on.

For the first time I was able to read something about someone who said things that I could identify with. At the same time I also read about the way she had been treated and what had happened once her story was known. I got a glimpse of the general reaction of people in Britain when it came to transsexuals and it wasn't very nice. Despite the fact that she had been a successful model and was very obviously a woman, I got the impression that she was regarded as a freak by so many people.

I now realise just how difficult it must have been for her all those years ago. This was someone who, like me and most other transsexuals, knew from a very early age that they had been born into the wrong body. But she was born in 1935 and as difficult as it still is for the transgender community these days, it is nothing like it was then for her. She had her operation to fully transition in Morocco in 1960 after saving enough money from her job working at a Paris cabaret club, but because of the way the laws worked in the UK she only received her female birth certificate in 2005, a year after the Gender Recognition Act was passed. It's incredible to think that despite having fully transitioned 45 years earlier she was not allowed to be recognised as a woman in her own country until she was 70. April received the MBE in 2012 for her services to transgender equality and even had an exhibition dedicated to her a year later at the Museum of Liverpool, the city where she had been born into a family of six children. Hers is an amazing story.

Pioneering transsexuals like her were regularly described in ways that were always very derogatory and spiteful. I was left in no doubt what most people thought of them or anyone who did not conform to what people believed was sexually normal. Gays, transvestites, transsexuals – they were all lumped under the same umbrella and the general consensus of opinion in south London was that they were all a load of perverts.

I knew exactly what was expected of me as a young man and an apprentice chef making his way. There was no way I was going to do anything else other than fight the inner feelings I had. Without ever really thinking about it, I suppose the battle with those thoughts had been there throughout my young life. I was determined to defeat them.

CHAPTER FOUR

Liberated

I was still a relatively shy teenager and certainly nothing like the Frank Maloney the world would come to know later on in my life. I had to force myself to do a lot of the things my mates were doing because they didn't come naturally. Making sure I was part of the crowd was very important.

When it came to girls I was pretty shy, but I did like talking to them. My mates were always really after one thing with girls and that was very obviously sex. Lots of my friends had been early starters when it came to losing their virginity and they seemed so experienced when it came to the number of girls they'd been out with. I was a very slow starter. I'd chat to them when we went out to pubs and bars and I was really content with just doing that. I'm sure part of the reason for this was the way I felt in my head.

I was still having my dreams and in them I was still a girl. I was also dressing occasionally in women's clothes, usually my mum's, or those that had been left by my aunt in the cupboard.

I was always really careful to put them back in exactly the same place I had found them and to fold them in the same way they had been put away. Quite often after I did things like this I would go out and do something macho. I'd go out with my mates or play football. It seemed to help me blank out any feelings of guilt I might have been harbouring. It also meant that I didn't dwell on what was going on in my mind. The busier I stayed the less likely I was to start thinking about my gender identity. I was so desperate to be what I saw as normal, to have all the thoughts about wanting to be female disappear, but it had gone on for too long for it to be a passing phase. The question now was how to deal with it.

I remember bringing up the subject with my dad, probably when there was publicity in the papers about April Ashley and his reaction was to say that it wasn't normal. That was it. I knew then that I would never be able to talk to him about it again. I certainly didn't want him to think the same thing about his son and it was a really depressing moment. I knew whatever was inside me was going to have to remain a secret. I loved my dad and I knew he loved me, but I knew that revealing the way I felt was a step too far. Subconsciously, I think I made the decision it would never happen.

When I was out with mates and I looked at girls I did so in a very different way to them. There would be plenty of comments like, 'What would you like to do with her!', while I'd be think-ing that what the girls were wearing was really nice. My fear of being an outsider and not being part of the crowd never left me – it probably grew throughout my teenage years. There were some pretty nasty things going on in parts of London at the time if you stood out – either because of your sexual orientation or your colour.

It's not nice to recall it now but there were often reports of 'Paki-bashing', when Pakistani immigrants and other Asians had been picked on, as well as 'queer-bashing'. I remember there were a couple of gay guys who used to live near us and one of them was a drag artist. They would regularly walk their little white dog in the streets around where I lived and thankfully nobody ever did them any physical harm. In fact, everyone used to talk to them and people were very polite, at least to their faces. But I also heard all the comments which were made about them behind their backs and the way they were referred to as poofters or fairies. They might have been part of the local community but it was very clear to me that they were also outsiders simply because they were different.

Football remained one of my main escape routes. Any cares I might have had in the week seemed to drift away during a Saturday afternoon watching Millwall and joining in the banter with the other supporters on the terraces. I felt a real sense of bonding and I was almost part of another family. Most Saturday nights after matches we'd be out in clubs and pubs, drinking and chatting up girls, although I was never a really heavy drinker and I was more intrigued by the way girls acted.

When I was out in shops looking at clothes for myself, I always kept an eye on women's clothes and wished I could buy them instead. But even my male friends were interested in clothes shopping – looking good when you went out for the night was very important. A lot of time was spent in making sure you had the right clothes and that the girls would like your look. In that sense, my friends were just like so many other young guys growing up in working-class areas of London. The group I was part of went on to do all sorts of different things with their careers, like boxing, money broking and antique trading. There were a couple who ended up in prison for one thing or another, and there was also the sad case of one of our friends who committed suicide. We were always there for each other if there was ever any problems when we had our nights out.

Another reason for wandering around the West End was to visit certain places and shops that offered me the chance to discover more about the world I knew very little about, namely transsexuals. Soho catered for all sorts of tastes. Several shops sold various magazines relating to transsexuals on their shelves and it wasn't difficult to go in and have a browse. You could look at the magazines without buying them and give the impression that you were just looking without really knowing exactly what you wanted. I managed to read more about men who wanted to be women, but lots of the stories concentrated purely on the sexual aspect. I wanted to know more about the whole experience of someone who felt they had been born into the wrong body.

Sexually, I was a relatively late developer in comparison to the other guys I hung around with. When it came to thinking about intimacy I found myself imagining I was the woman. In my mind I started reversing the roles, imagining myself as the female and that seemed to help me when it came to getting aroused. But once again my need to fit in and not be seen as an outsider meant that I joined in with the rest of the boys – at least on the surface of things. The great thing was that if I spent the night talking to a girl and then we were both seen by everyone leaving together, the assumption was that I'd pulled a bird and was off somewhere having my wicked way with her. Quite often nothing could be further from the truth. It was simply that I enjoyed talking to the girls and asking them about their lives and what they got up to. I let the lads assume what they wanted and it didn't take much for their imaginations to go into overdrive. Was I interested in sex?

Yes, I was, just like any other young person, but I can't say it was something that I was obsessed with. Sex for the sake of it seemed a bit hollow. I think I was searching for something a bit more meaningful and when I was 17, I found it.

By this time I was boxing for the Fisher club in Bermondsey alongside Eugene and Tony Hudson. The three of us went to a dance that was being held at the football club they also played for. Like Eugene, Tony was never short of a word or two. They were characters and could be very funny and both of them looked and acted older than their age. Very much like each other in many ways. Not long after we arrived at the dance I saw a very pretty girl in hot pants hanging around with some of her friends. She was small, blonde and there was something about her that I found really attractive. She looked great and I immediately found myself wanting to talk to her. She told me her name was Jackie and it turned out she was Tony Hudson's sister. Peckham is a pretty small place and you tended to know a lot of the other young people in the area, but I'd never seen her before which was probably due to the fact that she was only 14. We talked quite a bit that night and arranged to see each other again. I thought she looked lovely and when we chatted I found her really easy to talk to. We got on well and laughed a lot which was a good sign. I was really keen to make sure we saw each other again. By this time I'd been out with a few girls but hadn't really had a serious relationship. Jackie seemed different somehow, I felt happy and comfortable in her company and, yes, there was a real attraction for me from the very first time my I set my eyes on her.

We began to see quite a bit of each other which meant I wasn't hanging around as much with my mates. I wasn't boxing quite as much as I had done either, but my career in the catering business was progressing well. I was based at the Adelphi Ministry of Defence building on the Strand and had also passed my City and Guilds exams. But Jackie's parents were not too keen on our relationship, they clearly didn't think I was right for her – and there was the question of our age difference. It's something I can understand now being a parent myself, but at the time I couldn't see what was wrong with the two of us going out together. We slowly began to drift apart and by the time I was offered the chance of a posting to Honiton in Devon, we really weren't going out together at all.

The job in Devon was based at a government-run camp for Asian refugees from Uganda. They had been made to leave the country by the dictator Idi Amin and Honiton was one of the camps that they used to house the displaced people. The new job was a step up from what I was doing in London. It was also good experience because the place was home to about 900 people and having to cater for them was a real challenge, especially when I inadvertently caused a near riot. I had what I thought was a brilliant idea of trying to involve the refugees in the catering for the camp as it would be really nice for them to have some home cooking. I invited some of the refugees to do the cooking and they produced some lovely dishes. The problem was that I somehow managed to mix up the Hindu and Muslim dishes, not realising the strict eating code which went with their religions. The result was arguments everywhere rather than a peaceful and happy meal. So much for my master plan. At one point there were also plates hurled through the air.

When I returned from Devon I found myself having to deal with some traumatic news. My parents had split up – a devastating blow for me. I think there had been signs that things weren't going well, although I can't honestly say that I remember how long it went on. There were instances that I have no recollection of at all now and I suspect I may have blanked them out of my mind because I was so upset at the two of them splitting up. There do seem to be gaps when I try to recall exactly what went on. I remember the air of tension in the house and that the two of them did have rows, but I had never believed it would come to them breaking up in the way they did. After spending the first 19 years of my life with a family background that seemed pretty normal, the whole thing was shattered in an instant.

My mother moved out of the house and I think she was on the verge of a nervous breakdown, while my dad was on a month's notice from the priest who was in charge of the property. From having what I had come to know as a secure family home, I was suddenly faced with the prospect of having nothing at all. I was 19, Eugene was off doing his own thing and my dad made the decision to move away. That meant I had to look for a place of my own and I decided to take my youngest brother, Vince, with me. He was still at school and I was happy to look after him – as soon as I found somewhere to go.

For a time I still lived at the house with my dad and I was aware that the cupboard my aunt used for the storage was still stocked full with women's clothes. Despite my relationship with Jackie, the inner feelings I had about wanting to be a woman hadn't disappeared. I may have done all sorts of macho things but I couldn't get away from the nagging feeling that I was functioning in the wrong body. I had suffered some kind of mistake at birth. I should have been born a female, but instead I had a male body with a mind that felt very uncomfortable with the body it had to function in. I found the more time I spent working and getting on with life, the less likely I was to think about my problem. It resurfaced at quiet times, as did the dreams.

I could go for days or weeks without having one, but then all of a sudden a dream would pop up, just as vivid as ever. They seemed to keep pace with my age as well. I was no longer the little girl I'd been when I was a young boy. Now I saw myself as a young woman and I'd be with other young women of my own age.

At home, the temptation to look in that cupboard full of women's clothes proved too much. I started putting them on again and I thought they looked nice as well as acting as an escape from the tension and the pressure of what had been happening between my mum and dad. I could lose myself in another world and feel relaxed. I was alone with my own thoughts and feelings and I felt comfortable with myself because I wasn't putting on an act. For those few moments I was being me.

Back at work, I got my first managerial position and moved to a new location in Gower Street in London. I enjoyed the extra responsibility and the fact that I seemed to be making progress in my career. But it couldn't help the numbness I felt after the break-up. I'm sure it was upsetting for both of my brothers as well, as the family unit was suddenly split up in all sorts of directions. I had a month before having to move out of the family house and I had to find somewhere else to live.

Gower Street was a pretty sociable place to work and I never had any problems making friends. Among them was a new guy who had started in the personnel department, Alan Ferris. I often used to pop into his tiny office for a chat, making myself at home as I sat back in a chair and put my feet up on his desk – he used to moan about it all the time, but tolerated me doing it and loved to talk. Not that he had too much choice because I would walk into his office whenever I felt like it. He was a larger-than-life character, very articulate and well-educated. He came from Wales but had gone to Goldsmiths college in New Cross, south London which was just around the corner from The Den. He knew all about Millwall and some of the places I'd grown up in as a kid. He loved the theatre and I could imagine him on stage booming out his lines with his exaggerated hand movements as he played all sorts of roles. He was very extrovert and had a bubbly and infectious personality. Although he never really mentioned it during any of our little chats in his office, he was also obviously gay, something I had no problem with at all and I'm sure he recognised that.

We talked about my parents splitting up and Alan told me he still hadn't really found anywhere permanent to live since moving to London. He suggested that we get somewhere together not too far from work and share the costs. When I thought about it, the idea not only made financial sense but I liked the prospect of sharing with someone I already knew and got on well with. He had no problem with having Vince stay. From being quite concerned about what I was going to do and where I was going to stay, I began to feel much more upbeat about the future.

Neither of us had great salaries and the cost of living in London wasn't cheap, even in those days. We had to be realistic about what we could afford and that meant we were limited to looking at some pretty grotty properties. In the end we settled on a flat in Highbury, north London, not too far from the old ground that used to be home to Arsenal. It was big enough for the three of us but apart from that it was a dump and I was amazed the landlady was allowed to rent it out. It was that bad – dirty and smelly when we arrived, with mice running around. The electricity was patchy, to say the least. When you had a bath in the evening you used candles for light, not for atmosphere. I felt so sorry for Vince because the shock must have hit him more than it did me. He was a fairly quiet boy and was still at school over in south

London, so it meant quite a trek each morning and afternoon for him. He also had to come to terms with the familiarity and cosiness of his family home suddenly disappearing in front of his eyes.

Fortunately, Alan not only proved to be a really good person to share a home with but he was happy to help with looking after Vince. He was always upbeat and his personality helped us to stay happy. Alan loved to sing and he loved to play his soundtrack recordings of musicals like *Jesus Christ Superstar*. You couldn't stop him, and I actually liked hearing him around the flat because it took my mind off the dreary surroundings. At first I kept a bit of distance between us, but that didn't really last for long. He'd often be going out at night and I'd ask him where.

'Frank, I can't take you to these places I go to,' he told me once. 'You'd be shocked!'

Getting to know Alan better helped me to deal with my inner thoughts. For the first time in my young life – and with his encouragement and support – I began to try to be myself. I started to feel liberated because I was able to live with a sense of freedom. I suspect he might have recognised that there was something lurking beneath the surface with me, but he didn't know exactly what it was. He was not only a good talker but a good listener as well and he was also a naturally funny man.

Alan was very open and not afraid to talk about his sexuality. It must have been difficult for anyone who was gay then, although things had definitely improved compared to ten or 15 years earlier. Seeing him get on with his life and not care a damn about what anyone else thought was really interesting. Here was someone who was not afraid to be who he really was while I was afraid to own up to who and what I was.

Without there being any one moment I gradually began to open up to Alan and explain the way I felt. It was a relief to finally be able to talk about some of the things that had been going on in my mind for as long as I could remember. Somehow I knew I could trust Alan and felt comfortable talking to him about the fact that I often felt I was a girl trapped in a boy's body. How I'd had dreams since I was a kid where I would always be a girl and how I liked women's clothes and wished I could dress in them. Not once during our conversations did I feel Alan was judging me or telling me what I felt was wrong. Instead, he told me to be myself and give in to the feelings I had rather than try to fight them. Alan's views and the lifestyle he already led were very different to mine and the background I came from. He moved in very different circles to the ones I'd inhabited back in Peckham, and with his help and encouragement I began to live a second sort of life. One I had never experienced until then, and which helped me to feel happier and more contented than I had been before.

Alan was probably the first gay guy I'd ever really properly met and he slowly began to introduce me to a very different sort of lifestyle that I knew nothing about. He was incredibly flamboyant and extrovert, and there's no doubt some of the confidence he displayed helped me to have the courage to explore more about the way I felt. I wanted to know about what had been going on in my head throughout my life. I didn't want to feel like a freak and I knew there were plenty of people out there who felt like me. Alan helped me to have the courage to be myself and was also someone I could talk to and he was happy for me to ask him questions. To be honest, it was a relief to be able to relax and talk with another human being without worrying about how I would be judged and whether I would be seen as a complete outsider.

My state of mind was reflected in the way I looked. I started to let my hair grow and it wasn't long before I had flowing locks. Men's fashion in the 1970s had moved on in leaps and bounds.

We'd gone through all the upheaval and change in the swinging '60s, with the explosion of colour in both women's and men's clothes. In many ways the styles for both sexes were now merging, with long, flowing shirts, flared trousers, boots with big heels and long hair all commonplace for young men. The clothes I wore for work could have looked good on men or women and it was all perfectly acceptable but I also went a little further at weekends and when going out in the evening.

I was very careful not to let Vince hear or see things I didn't want him to. He has since told me that he felt there was something a bit different going on during the time he lived with me but he was never fully aware of what I was doing. When it came to female clothes, I made sure they were kept well hidden and only wore them when he wasn't around. I sometimes dressed when I was in the flat and being able to put on women's clothes and feel relaxed about it was a tremendous relief. Alan had talked to me about transvestites and how some men just liked dressing as women but in terms of their sexual preference they still liked women and often had perfectly normal sex lives with females. I instinctively knew I wasn't a transvestite. Dressing as a woman wasn't about me getting a sexual kick, either. It was all about my gender. The more I thought about it the more I knew I wanted to be a woman and not a man.

I was drifting away from my Peckham life – I even stopped going to watch Millwall. Living away from home allowed me to make a new start. I'm not sure I consciously decided not to see my old friends, it just happened. A lot of it was down to the circumstance of not living in south London any more. Having Alan there to talk to was certainly a help. I told him all about my family and my dreams and mentioned the fact that when I went to bed at night I would often wish that by some miracle or other I would wake up in the morning and be a girl. He was sympathetic and said that I could be whatever I wanted to be. It was good to hear those words of encouragement and it helped me to start to think differently about the way I could live my life.

I dressed as a female – when Vince wasn't around – and would go out fully dressed as a woman. Alan took me on my first visit to a pub as a woman, to the Lord Nelson in Holloway Road. I wore long, flowing skirts, platform shoes, nice feminine tops, I carried a handbag and also used touches of make-up. I didn't feel strange; I felt comfortable and happy to be dressed as a woman. After all, I'd dreamed about being a girl for as long as I could remember. We went to places like Leicester Square, out to the shops or to go for something to eat. I did normal, everyday things, but I was doing it as a woman and it felt very natural. Alan told me not to be frightened by the thoughts I had of being a woman. His awareness of what I was going through helped me.

My circle of friends changed as well. I became quite friendly with a couple of girls at work and they would sometimes pop over to the flat, although they never saw me fully dressed as a woman. They were used to the sort of clothes I wore to the office and although we got on really well I never told them about my feelings of wanting to be totally female. I never felt I could fully open up to them.

As I worked for the civil service there was often a crossover with other branches and I came into contact with a couple of page boys and girls who worked at Buckingham Palace. We'd go out and have drinks together from time to time, and suddenly I found myself with a whole new set of friends, although I never dressed as a woman when I was with them. I suppose you could say that I kind of dressed between the lines, because that's exactly what you could do back then. Platform boots, a long coat, flared jeans and even a bit of eye make-up wasn't out of the ordinary for guys. I was very small and slight and even got mistaken for a girl a couple of times when I was travelling on trains. I never corrected them. I actually quite enjoyed it.

When I did go out dressed in female clothes I was passable and never got stared at or had the feeling that people saw me as a man dressed up as a woman. They just thought I was a girl and that was it. Alan took me to a club once where there were transvestites and some transsexuals. I was mortified when I looked at some of them because they just looked like men dressed up as women and it certainly wasn't what I wanted, but my interest in the whole subject started to grow. The trouble was that a lot of what I read came from places like sex shops in Soho and they had nothing to do with the practical side of the subject. I came across stories of people who called themselves shemales, which effectively meant they were half and half when it came to their gender. There was no way I wanted to be like them. Then I read about transvestites and had to ask myself if perhaps that was really what I was, even though I had been sure I wasn't. Maybe I just like putting on women's clothing? I asked myself again. But then why did I have the sort of dreams I'd had since I was a kid when I was always a real girl in them? The more I read, the more confused I became.

At least I didn't have any real responsibility, apart from looking after Vince and that wasn't really a problem. Once he'd finished with school he got himself a job as an apprentice hairdresser with Vidal Sassoon. He began to be more independent and had his own life to lead, so my whole existence at that time was quite relaxed. I'll never know how my life may have turned out had I continued to live there and carry on leading the lifestyle

I'd created for myself, but I didn't – and the main reason for that was an unexpected phone call. I instantly recognised the voice on the other end of the line. It was my Dad and I immediately panicked.

CHAPTER FIVE

Taking it on the nose

The phone call from my dad took me completely by surprise. It had been more than 18 months since my parents split up and I hadn't had any contact with my father during that time or with my mother. After they split up it was as if the family just went their separate ways. I didn't fall out with my mother or father, but we just seemed to drift apart. It wasn't that I never expected to hear from him again, but hearing his voice jolted me back to the life I'd led before moving to the flat. Things had changed a lot for me during my time away from Peckham and yet within seconds of picking up the phone and hearing my dad's voice I felt myself being drawn back into the Frank I was before my parents' break-up.

Dad told me that he wanted to see me and also asked if it would be possible for him to come and stay with us for a while. It was such a shock to hear from him that my head was spinning by the time I put the receiver down. Of course I wanted to see him, and of course I told him there would be no problem with him coming to stay, but once we'd finished the conversation, I lost my cool.

I couldn't let him see me the way I usually appeared, even though I didn't look any different to other young guys. I remember thinking, what will my dad think when he knows I'm sharing a flat with a gay guy? What will he think of the clothes I've been wearing? By the time we met, I'd had my hair cut and got rid of the clothes I was convinced he'd disapprove of. But dad got on well with Alan and thanked him for helping me to look after Vince.

He wanted to know what had been going on in my life and I gave him the – edited – highlights. There was no way I was going to tell him the full story about the way I'd been dressing and some of the things I'd been up to socially but he was really pleased to hear that I was moving up the ladder in my catering career. I told him that I hadn't been going to Millwall and explained that I had kind of moved on from friends in south London. I think he was a bit disappointed that I'd stopped boxing and it wasn't too long before I went out and found a new boxing club. Dad didn't have anywhere to live at the time and asked if he would be able to stay with us. It wasn't exactly what I'd expected, but I certainly wasn't going to say 'No', and Alan didn't have any objections.

I will always credit my dad with being the driving force in my life. He made me want to achieve something because that was always what he'd drummed into me and my brothers. But when he came back into my life I felt that we were on a different wavelength and there were times when I wanted to tell him I was different – except I just couldn't do it. I think it was the fear of letting him down as our relationship had changed and I got the feeling he respected me more. I think there was a certain pride that I was doing well at work and around this time I went to work for the

Inland Revenue at Somerset House as a restaurant manager. The basic salary was good and my pay was performance-related.

I still had my dreams even though I prayed I wouldn't. If anything, they became more intense, waking me up in the middle of the night and leaving me unable to get back to sleep. I would walk around the flat telling myself that this was not what I wanted. What I wanted was a normal life. I still had the desire to be a woman and often wished I had been born female – but I hadn't. I'd kept stories about April Ashley and would avidly read any news about transsexuals but I never wanted to be the subject of a story in a paper in the way that they were. I wanted to be the same and to blend in. Would I have felt like this had my father not re-entered my life when he did? Who knows? Perhaps it would have been totally different for me and I would have had the courage to be myself earlier in my life instead of waiting for nearly 40 years. I think that the longer I'd stayed in my female mode back then the more likely it would have been for me to have transitioned, but I will never know. I don't know what my father would have said if I'd told him, 'Dad, I'm really a girl, I want to have a sex change.' It wasn't just the fear of what my dad would have said, but also what others might have thought. It was easier to just go on denying my real self. Within a very short period of time I found myself slipping back into being the old Frank Maloney.

I got on with my new job, I went out occasionally to some of the old places I used to frequent and getting back into boxing meant I was doing a lot of the things I had done before moving to north London. I have to admit that boxing and training felt really good, although getting whacked in the face was never something that I liked or got used to. Once again I was looking very much like a typical working-class bloke.

I'd been told by someone I used to hang around with back in Peckham that Jackie had asked about me and so I gave him my number to pass on. I had never forgotten her and when we spoke on the phone for the first time in two years I remembered how special it had been when we first met. There had been a desire on my part to be seen to be a normal young guy, but going out with Jackie hadn't really fallen into that category. I was really taken with her and we got on well. I could sense there was still something there between us and when I later met her for a date I realised I was right.

I had been running regular discos at Somerset House on Friday nights and inviting her to one was the perfect way of meeting again. When she turned up she looked just as pretty as I remembered her and we seemed to pick up where we had left off. There was a bit of catching up to do – which I glossed over for my part – but it turned out that she was due to be getting married to another guy. It was funny, but I immediately felt I didn't want her to do it. I don't think I was jealous. Maybe I was being competitive and not wanting the feeling that someone else had beaten me to her, but I had a pretty strong feeling that her marriage wasn't going to happen. She ended up coming back to the flat where we talked some more. In fact, she stayed the night and, by the time morning rolled around, Jackie's plans to get married no longer existed.

We began seeing each other again and it wasn't too long before her parents found out. They hadn't been keen on me the first time around and nothing had changed in their eyes, they just didn't like the idea of their daughter seeing me. As far as they were concerned I wasn't the right person for Jackie, particularly as she had been set to marry someone else. Her mother made it clear that she either stopped seeing me immediately or she could find somewhere else to live. Jackie bravely ended up moving in with me at the flat just before Christmas 1974. My dad had found himself a place but our flat was still in a pretty awful condition. She never complained and just got on with things. She even got a new job that was closer to home. Everything we did seemed to happen very quickly. I'd already arranged to be in Scotland over the holiday period and I just took off and left her there in the flat alone. Alan was also away for Christmas. As you might imagine, Jackie had a miserable time and we were on the phone a lot, but I couldn't just get on a train and get back to London until after Boxing Day.

As soon as I returned to London I knew exactly what to do. I went straight from the station to a second-hand jewellers in the Holloway Road, bought a ring for £50, went to the flat and asked Jackie to marry me. We decided we wanted the wedding to happen quickly and on 14 January 1975 we were married at the local registry office. We had a lunch at the Adelphi in London – where I had once worked – and it was paid for by my employers. The reception was a hastily arranged affair and both my mum and dad were there as well as my brothers, but we didn't tell Jackie's parents.

My employers gave me £100 which we used to go to Salisbury, although the hotel wouldn't give us a room at first because the owner thought the pair of us looked far too young to be a honeymooning couple! We knew that when we got back from Salisbury we would have to let Jackie's parents know that their daughter was not only married, but married to the man they clearly hadn't wanted. When Jackie got in touch her mum told her it was probably about time that she came home, little knowing her daughter had got married. Jackie explained why she wouldn't be taking her mother up on the offer and I don't think it went down at all well. It wasn't a great reaction, but there wasn't very much she could do about it.

I was now a married man. I had taken yet another step along the 'normal bloke' path. The speed and excitement of getting married had occupied my thoughts since getting back with Jackie. There was no doubt I was attracted to her and I think I loved her as well. But we were still really just kids who hadn't taken their time to have a long relationship before deciding to get married. Both of us were going down a very traditional route very quickly and not for the first or last time in my life I got caught up in the moment.

CHAPTER SIX

Small, blonde and pretty

I hadn't given any real thought to my gender problem and the effect it might have on my relationship with Jackie. I suspect I hoped getting married might finally banish my female urges forever. We managed to get ourselves a new home in Ealing and not long after moving across to west London, Jackie became pregnant. I was delighted. It wasn't about my desire to appear normal to the outside world, it just felt lovely to know that I was going to be a father and have a family of my own. But it was true that I was now going to seem even more normal and traditional. The reality was that my gender problem never went away. I just fought hard to keep it under lock and key.

I was busy at work, we were a newly married couple with a child on the way and in my spare time I was still boxing as an amateur. I'd started to consider turning professional in order to earn a bit of extra cash. It was all quite exciting in a way and because things were happening fast, I just seemed to get caught up in the moment and went along with the course my life was taking. Jackie and I must have seemed like the perfect couple. We were even about the same height. Jackie was small, blonde and very pretty. It was a look that was to take my eye over the years whenever I saw a girl who fitted that image. I think part of the reason was perhaps I saw in her what I would want to look like. Looking at myself in a mirror had always been depressing for me. I didn't like what was looking back at me. When I'd had a dream during the night and seen myself as a girl, looking in the mirror the next morning and seeing Frank was unsettling. Being small, blonde and pretty would have fitted the bill.

When the day of the birth arrived we panicked. I didn't drive and so a neighbour had to take us to hospital. Word had got out that Jackie had gone into labour and suddenly there were family and friends at the hospital causing chaos, but by that evening, 14 February 1976, Emma was born. It was a lovely moment and I felt genuinely blessed to have become a father. When I first saw little Emma I could never have imagined just how important she would be to me and the role she would play in my life. Alan – my former flatmate who also got on well with Jackie – seemed the perfect person to be godfather and happily he was delighted to accept the invitation.

I remember holding Emma up to the window in the hospital to give her a glimpse of the world that was waiting outside for her and then giving her a big kiss. I also kissed Jackie, saying that I'd see her the next day, and then went out to wet the baby's head. I was gone for three days.

My lost days are not something that I'm proud about but it just happened and it was part of the world I had gone back into. Having a drink with your mates was the accepted thing when you became a father, but I have to admit that I took it a bit too far when it came to the celebrations. I also sampled more exotic establishments than the pubs I went to with south London friends.

One of Somerset House's suppliers was Courage, the brewers, and some of the guys from the company decided to take me out for the night. They obviously had lots of clients all over London and not all of them were in the pub trade. They told me they were going to take me to a club that they thought was special and said we'd have a great time. The place was full of very attractive women, chatting and drinking with men. It was pretty clear that the women were hostesses, but what wasn't clear to me as I sat down and made myself comfortable was that all the women were in fact men.

When the man from Courage told me I didn't believe him at first. My only thought as I'd walked through the door was just how stunning some of the women looked. The guy from Courage said that the club was one of their best accounts. I was in awe because I wasn't aware this sort of club existed. I began talking to one of the girls and although I was a bit drunk, I can still remember just how good-looking she was. She was very slim and wore a pink dress with a slit up the side. The transvestite that ran the place was quite big and buxom and wasn't as good-looking. The girl I talked to told me that some of the hostesses were on hormones, but it didn't really mean too much to me at the time. Now I realise that there must have been some girls there who were probably going to fully transition while others seemed content to dress as woman.

Nobody paid any notice to me talking to the girl in the pink dress and the men from Courage had doubtless seen the same reaction from other people they had taken there. I was absolutely fascinated by the whole place and the thought that there must have been girls there who had the same thing going on in their minds as me. I couldn't help thinking about their strange world and how they went about their lives working as hostesses in a club every night. Men but not men, women but not women. I wondered what they were exactly and I wondered what exactly I was.

I did know for certain that I was a married man who now had a baby daughter. I wanted to be a good husband and a good father. That was my role. That was what had been drummed into me throughout my life. I wanted to be successful at work and provide for them, I wanted to achieve something with my life. I wanted to be Frank Maloney and I could sort my mind out, I could manage things and I could be in charge of my life.

When I eventually turned up at the hospital feeling guilty and ready to take the ear-bashing that Jackie would be justified in dishing out, the first person I saw was a giant of a man called Guy Williamson, one of my boxing club mates who remains a true friend to this day. He was then a friendly heavyweight, weighing around 18 stone, and he was sitting at Jackie's bedside holding a massive pink toy elephant. It was a funny sight, although Guy had been kind enough to visit Jackie in the hospital while I'd gone on the missing list. Some of the other mums thought he must be the father.

Guy won all sorts of titles as an amateur boxer in the super-heavyweight category and had a long and distinguished career as a senior police officer before becoming a barrister about 13 years ago. He is still the big, friendly person I've always known and he and his wife, Hazel, are lovely people. Their kindness and support in more recent times was very important to me.

Jackie's parents had been told about Emma's arrival and the birth eventually helped lead to their rift being healed. Having a family felt good and I was determined to make sure everything worked out. We moved to a maisonette in Leytonstone and I also got myself a new job not too far away, working as an assistant catering manager for an American bank in Stratford. I loved having Emma around and she would spend a lot of time with me. I'd take her everywhere and even used to have her with me at work on occasions where she'd play happily in a corner for hours on end. The job at the bank was good, but I was always trying to find ways of making a bit of extra money. I again considered trying to turn professional after answering an advertisement in *Boxing News*. But any hopes of me turning pro and becoming a champion soon disappeared when I found out about some of the problems I might have trying to make any real money. I only weighed around 8st and in the lighter weight categories fighters simply weren't paid that much, so I began to look at other avenues for extra money.

Once I'd finally passed my driving test I hit upon the idea of starting a home gardening business with a bit of help from my dad and a neighbour called Paddy Doyle. I placed adverts in the local paper and we had more jobs than we could cope with. Dad and Paddy used to do all the work and on the one occasion I decided to get my hands dirty by using a Rotavator I ended up churning through a woman's prized roses by mistake. I managed to get out of the mess I'd created by telling her they all had greenfly and it would have caused her terrible problems with the rest of the garden if I hadn't got rid of them. In the end she was so pleased with my piece of initiative that she gave us a bonus.

I changed jobs once more when my former boss at Somerset House offered me the opportunity to become responsible for catering at the Department for Health and Social Security offices at the Elephant and Castle, which meant a welcome move back to south London. And we more than doubled our money when we sold the flat in Leytonstone. Jackie's parents took over as land-lords at a pub in Deptford called The Duke of Wellington. It was in one of the roughest areas of south London, but when the two of them asked if we'd like to run it for them there was no hesita-tion on our part. I fancied a change and was bored with the day-to-day running of a restaurant.

The pub was very near to one owned by a famous local char-acter called Harry Hayward who you didn't mess around with. Happily for us, he seemed to like me and one day he came into our pub unannounced, closed the doors behind him and then told all the local lads that if anyone took liberties with us they would answer to him. He told them all to treat Jackie and me with respect and we never had any trouble, despite the fact that there were some real nutcases who used to come in for a drink. Like lots of blokes they liked a game of darts, except their game had a twist. They would take their shirts off and stand in front of the board so that they could throw darts at each other's backs.

The pub was a crazy place but mostly good-natured, although I could tell some of the antics made Jackie a bit uneasy and one particular incident spooked us both. I was upstairs one even-ing when there was a bit of an altercation between some guys in the bar. The next morning I saw a body being dragged out of the water at Deptford Creek bridge and it didn't take me long to recognise that it was one of the men who had been arguing the night before. Jackie began to feel more uncomfortable about be-ing there and eventually her parents decided to sell the place and buy another pub in Sussex.

We already had a home in Orpington which we moved back into and I got a job at Bromley college as their catering manager, but I had developed a taste for the pub life. Being in charge and being on show to the customers appealed to something in my character.

I boxed with my brother Eugene at the Trinity club near the Elephant and Castle and our trainer was a guy called Billy King-well. It was because of Billy that I got involved in training some of the youngsters. I really enjoyed it and before long I'd passed a training course and took my first steps to earning my living from the sport. I could now be paid by the local council for the two nights each week that I was at the club. I also worked as a mini-cab driver on Thursday, Friday and Saturday nights, but I became more involved with the Trinity club and found I had a natural ability to organise boxing matches for shows at a working men's club in the Old Kent Road. I staged a fight that involved a young south Londoner named Frank Bruno who fought an Irish boxer called Joe Christle – the only time Frank lost as an amateur.

I liked amateur boxing but if I wanted to try and make some money from the sport then it was the professional side of the game that I needed to be looking at. Eventually I became a pro-fessional trainer but it certainly didn't mean I could give up my day job. By this time, I'd stopped working at Bromley college, we'd sold our house in Orpington, and we moved in with Vince and his wife who had a place in Strood, Kent.

I'd opened a greengrocer's in the Blackfriars, London. I was working non-stop, taking boxers all over the country at night af-ter working all day in the shop and then the next morning I would be at Spitalfields market getting all the fresh produce to stock the shop. Quite often I would go without sleep for 24 hours or just snatch a few minutes here and there. I was a workaholic and quite literally didn't have time to think, which was just the way I liked it.

CHAPTER SEVEN

Cover up

There was something about the life of being a pub landlord which I had liked. The chance came along to have our own pub and we took it, becoming the licensees of The Castle in Aldgate. It was pretty rundown when we took charge but it didn't take much working out that it could be successful. Aldgate is in east London and the pub was right on the fringes of a part of the city which was really taking off. I knew it had great potential if we put the work in.

Having the pub probably fitted in better with working as a trainer. I didn't have the worry of flying around trying to look after the greengrocer's while at the same time trying to look after fighters, one of whom was Eugene. It probably also helped that Jackie and I had something to focus on. We weren't exactly having problems with our marriage, but there was no doubt it could be explosive at times between us. There was never any one particular thing which caused problems and I don't know how much of this might have been due to my inner feelings which I was still trying to keep a lid on. We had rushed into getting married, we were both young and might have benefited from taking things more slowly.

I had to be strong in myself anyway and control whatever urges might suddenly sweep over me. It wasn't easy and there were times when I just couldn't stop what was going on in my head. When Jackie was out I would sometimes stare in the wardrobe at her clothes, feeling a desire to touch and wear them. I would sometimes pick up some of her clothes and hold them. That would be enough. It was almost as if it relieved some kind of tension. I sometimes tried on the clothes and looked at myself in the mirror and then I'd be all right. But there were other times when I looked in the mirror and tears would fill my eyes because seeing myself like that just made me ask that same question. Why wasn't I born a girl? I'd feel guilty because I was doing something behind Jackie's back, but I knew I could never tell her. I could never tell anyone, so I just had to keep it bottled up.

We gradually began to make progress with the pub, sorting it out and making it the kind of place that was well used both at lunchtimes and in the evenings. It was also useful because it was big enough to have one of the rooms on the first floor converted into a gym for the boxers I was helping to train. On the face of it, everything looked good. I'd got my professional trainer's licence and was looking after quite a few fighters. But then the whole thing fizzled out and for a time I fell out of love with boxing. I also went a little crazy when it came to my social life, going out regularly and drinking too much, which obviously didn't help my marriage. In the end Jackie moved out of the pub. Emma stayed with me but it wasn't a great situation and both my parents let me know in no uncertain terms exactly how they felt about the way I was carrying on.

After some more arguments and a couple of meetings, Jackie and I did eventually get back together but the atmosphere wasn't great and there were some very rocky patches as we tried to keep the marriage together. I suppose we both felt it was important for Emma to have her parents around, but there was no denying the unease that had crept into my relationship with Jackie.

The pub was still going well and I liked trying to introduce different things for the customers. One of them was a car rally with teams of men and women. The idea was that you went on a circuit and had clues at different stops that would tell you where to go next. The only problem was that we found ourselves with one person short for the women's team, so I suggested to Jackie that I partner her and dress up as a girl. I think she was a bit sceptical about the whole thing at first and clearly didn't think I could pull it off, but I insisted I was small and slight enough to get away with it.

We went shopping in the Mile End Road for a wig that we could have properly fitted and which would look good on me and then had to decide on the way we would dress. All the competitors had a theme to the way they dressed and we ended up wearing black tights, black shoes, black leotards and black tailcoats. Jackie did my make-up and I wore a pair of sunglasses. She insisted on me not saying a word during the course of the day, in case my voice gave me away. I was introduced as a friend of Jackie's and although all the people taking part that day were regulars at the pub, not one of them recognised me. We even ended up winning but once we told everyone who I was, they disqualified us! Everyone had a laugh but nobody knew just how much I had actually enjoyed the experience. I'd spent the whole day dressed entirely as a woman and I loved it.

I can't say I was being tortured by any inner feelings I was having at the time. Yes, in my quiet moments I might have had thoughts about my female feelings, but they were being kept in check mainly by keeping busy and leading a normal life. I think I had come to accept my thoughts as a part of me, as part of what I was but I was able to keep a lid on things.

I had the pub and my social life which kept me busy and I wasn't really missing boxing, but one day my father arrived with a friend of his. The friend knew that I'd been involved in boxing and told me his daughter's boyfriend was keen to turn professional. He wanted to ask me who I could recommend as a possible manager. I was happy to talk things through with them and I came up with a few names but then my father suggested that it would be a good idea for me to take out a manager's licence and look after the kid myself. After all, I'd trained boxers before, both amateurs and professionals, and I'd been involved in the sport since I was a youngster. Once I'd thought about the prospect it began to appeal to me. I was young and ambitious, with bags of energy – why not try my luck in a sport I knew and had grown up in? It was 1983 when I got my licence from the British Boxing Board of Control. The boxer I was going to manage was a lovely guy named Richie Edwards and, like so many fighters, he continued to combine his career in the ring with his day job – in his case, working as a dustman.

After four fights Ritchie decided to call it a day as a professional. At least he retired unbeaten in his short career, winning three contests and drawing one. His brief experience really made an impression on me. I loved every minute of being his manager, and it didn't take me long to start getting heavily involved in the sport once again. I immersed myself in the business and I think it came along at a good time for me. Running the pub was one thing, but I've always been a bit restless and I probably needed something like boxing to pour my energy into. I didn't realise it at the time, but Ritchie Edwards would be the first in a long line of boxers I would go on to manage or promote, in the process my life would change dramatically – and I became locked into being Frank Maloney.

CHAPTER EIGHT

Being Frank

I knew that boxing could be a tough business to break into, but that didn't worry me. I had confidence in my own ability to be a success, I had drive and bundles of energy. Getting my teeth stuck into a new project has always been something that has excited me and it was no different when it came to boxing. Very soon I was not only managing fighters but had formed a promotional company with a partner and began putting on shows around south London. I very soon realised not only that you had to work hard when it came to managing and promoting boxers, but you also had to make sure people took notice of what you were doing. The old saying about needing to put bums on seats was particularly true when you were promoting boxing contests in small venues like local town halls and I started to do a lot of them.

I might have been a shy kid but there was no way you could ever survive in boxing as a manager or particularly as a promoter if you were the shy, retiring type. I honestly don't think I was a natural at it, but I pushed myself now that was what was needed for the job. I would work 24 hours a day once we had announced a promotion to make sure that people knew about the show and bought tickets for it. I'd never sat at a table in front of reporters and cameras before but when I first had to do it I just got on with it. I'm sure I was a lot more self-conscious and less confident then, but I did it just the same and I would also know how to work the media when it came to getting publicity from them. I would always try to have an angle for them to write about and always be available for a quote. I'd do pretty much anything to sell my fighter. I realised the media had a job to do and that if you made it easier for them to do that job, you were likely to get the sort of coverage you wanted. It also helped that I genuinely liked the reporters and they seemed to like me. I was happy to have a drink and a chat with them and it wasn't too long before I had a bit of a profile. I think I was seen as this fresh-faced tough little cockney character.

I would be the one sitting at those press conferences talking up the various contests and telling anyone who was happy to listen just how good our promotion was. I loved it. I recognised very quickly the need to sell boxing. It required good, old-fashioned hard work and I'd always been happy to do that. I don't think the image was something I thought about. It just happened. I was being me and in doing so I suppose they might have seen a bit of a likeable Jack-the-lad character. I certainly wasn't going to destroy the image. There were often stories about me that did no harm at all. Like the time I stuck a hat pin into the backside of a 6-foot 5-inch heavyweight in order to make him get off his stool for the next round of a fight. It worked, by the way, because he won the contest.

I believed I could manage the situation, that any female urges I might have would be kept buried and not cause me any trouble.

I knew there was a life out there for me as Frank Maloney, doing the things that were expected of him, and I knew I had to get on with it and live that life. I wasn't upset about that. I was excited with what was going on in my working life and that was enough to suppress any other thoughts.

The pub went well for the next few years, making decent money and subsidising the boxing. But small-hall promoting can be costly when you are trying to build the business and in the end my accountant made me realise I was in trouble because boxing had become a drain on my finances. By this time we owned a cottage in Maidstone and decided that selling the property and moving to a new pub might be the best way to sort out my finances.

We left The Castle and moved in to a pub in Stanford-le-Hope in Essex for about seven months before a disagreement with the brewery saw us moving to a pretty rundown establishment in Kent called The Crayford Arms. I could see it had potential if it was run in the right way so we took it, aiming to build the trade in the same way we had done at The Castle. I was determined not to make the same mistakes again by using profits we made in the pub to help fund my promotions.

Luckily, I was approached by two of boxing's real old guard, Mike Barrett and Mickey Duff, which meant I didn't need to risk my own money. They wanted me to matchmake for them. I had to match boxers of various weights against each other to form the contests that would make up the poromotion on their shows. It was a great opportunity to gain more experience in boxing and I realised that to have success I needed good fighters, whether I was a manager or promoter. If you had a good fighter it was possible to build the business around them and if you had a really good boxer then the sky was the limit. The trick was finding the right fighter at the right time.

I got to take part in very big promotions, including a fight be-tween Nigel Benn and Michael Watson staged in a circus-style tent in Finsbury Park, London, on a warm Sunday evening in May 1989. It wasn't staged by Barrett and Duff but it was a massive event with weeks of publicity and big viewing figures when it was shown live in the UK and transmitted in the USA. The atmos-phere in the tent was electrifying and I got a real buzz, although I knew that events that big didn't come along too often. Benn lost but remained one of the best-known sportsmen around. The fight is still one of the most memorable nights I've had in boxing, but thanks to a phone call I had received from Las Vegas three months earlier, I was about to enter a period in my life in which I was to have many more.

CHAPTER NINE

The world at my feet

In early 1989 I got a phone call from a sports photographer called Lawrence Lustig who was in Las Vegas, USA, to cover a world welterweight title fight between Lloyd Honeyghan from the UK and an American named Marlon Starling. I'd known Lawrence for some time, he knew I was ambitious and always on the look-out for a potential champion. February was a big month for British fighters in Las Vegas – Frank Bruno fought Mike Tyson. Neither Brit ended up as winners, but it was another UK fighter that Lawrence phoned me about named Lennox Lewis.

With such a busy fight schedule in Vegas many of the sport's biggest players were in attendance. Lewis, who had won the Olympic super-heavyweight gold medal the year before in Seoul, was being courted by some of the most powerful people in boxing because he was about to turn professional. He was a very hot property and although he'd won his medal representing Canada at the Games, Lawrence reminded me that Lewis had, in fact, been born in the East End of London but had left when he was 12. He could become a huge sporting hero in the UK if he was handled and promoted in the right way. The question was how was I going to persuade the champion to ignore the likes of Don King and sign for little old me? The odds were heavily stacked against me, but I wasn't going to let that put me off.

I've been blessed with a natural desire to succeed and a very competitive streak. The more I thought about the prospect of signing Lennox Lewis, the more excited I became. After the initial shock of the call wore off, I realised there was no way I was going to be able to pull this thing off on my own. Lewis was in the position of being able to pick and choose, and I knew he'd never heard of me. Why should he have done? I was just a small-hall promoter from south London. At least Lawrence and his reporter colleague Ken Gorman were telling him that I was a young, up-and-coming manager from London. I knew that my best chance of convincing Lewis that he should begin his professional career in the country of his birth was to get him to London. I finally got hold of Lennox's lawyer, John Hornewer and got the two of them to agree to come over and meet me.

I had to sort out their air fares and the accommodation when they got to London, but that was the easy bit. Then I had to put together a package that would at least make me competitive. Through a series of phone calls with my most useful contacts, I managed to speak with a highly successful financial advisory company, the Levitt Group, that was said to be worth some £150 million. Boss Roger Levitt specialised in pensions and insurance and had set up a company called Olympic Gold hoping to compete with the sports agency IMG. I met with ex-footballer John Hollins and Charles Meaden from Olympic Gold, and I got on really well with Meaden. He was an old Harrovian and about the only thing we had in common was the fact that we were both the same sort of age, but he was easy to talk to him and could see the potential in what I was saying. Boxing was not something they had yet been involved in but Olympic Gold were willing to back my idea of signing Lennox Lewis and wanted me to bring along all the boxers I looked after.

I was given an annual consultancy fee, agreed a percentage from all fighters I signed for them, received a new Mercedes, my own offices in west London and a mobile phone. The most important part was making sure that I could convince Lennox I was the right person to guide his career as a professional boxer. I met Lewis and Hornewer at Heathrow, and immediately saw that Lennox had the calm and assured air of someone who was very confident. I felt very excited about the prospect of working with someone as talented as him. The negotiations went well, but I knew we were going to have to come up with something huge in order to tempt him to sign as he flew back to America.

Not long after, I met Roger Levitt for the first time. He walked around the office as if he were paying a royal visit. He was quite small with sharp features, slicked-back hair and a Groucho Marx moustache. He was holding a huge cigar and dressed in an expensive looking dark suit with a bow tie. He clearly liked to let everyone know he was the boss, and he also seemed to want to show he was a dynamic sort of person. He told me that I had to go out and sign Lewis, whatever it took to get the deal done. If it meant jumping on a plane that night, that's what I had to do. Very soon after our conversation I had my first taste of trans-Atlantic travel as I jetted off to New York to meet Lennox once more. I was determined to fly home as his manager. I eventually I got an agreement in place and it was decided Lennox would travel to London in April 1989 to sign the deal.

The day marked the culmination of 12 weeks' non-stop work. But what many in the business had believed was impossible had been made possible. I was going to be managing the hottest boxing prospect on the planet. By the morning I went to the airport with Emma to meet Lennox, I had lost 16 pounds, having existed on a terrible diet of snacks and ice cream, but when we had the press conference to announce the signing, my life changed. I was Frank Maloney, manager of Lennox Lewis. Nothing was ever going to be quite the same again.

The story of the signing was massive. The scale I was now going to be operating on was totally different. I'd been used to facing the press for quite a few years, but mainly in a small room with just a dozen or so reporters and a few photographers. At the Lewis conference I looked quite nervous and sheepish, very unlike the way I acted in the years that followed. The 12 weeks leading up to that day may have been busy, but the 12 years that were to follow were every bit their equal and they were also very exciting.

I threw myself into the job of making sure Lewis would one day become world heavyweight champion. I knew he was a class fighter and it was my job to try and map out his professional career so that he got the best possible opportunity of fulfilling the potential everyone knew he had. Did my female thoughts suddenly disappear at this time? No, but there was never any real time to dwell on them and they were kept in check by my busy career. I just got on with my life. There was always something going on and the buzz I got from the job was tremendous.

When I became Lennox's manager I was just 36 years old. It was a great opportunity and I was determined to put everything into the job. Boxing had been a part of my life since I first put gloves on as an 11-year-old. It was incredibly competitive and anyone involved in the sport needs to have their wits about them all the time. If you drop your guard as a boxer, you're going to get hit and if you drop your guard as a manager or promoter you will find yourself out of business. It was a tough old world but it was one in which I felt comfortable and confident in my own ability. There were plenty of snide comments from people in the game on both sides of the Atlantic but I expected that. I knew lots of them would do anything they could not only to undermine my reputation, but also to cast doubts in the mind of Lennox.

But Lewis was a smart guy who knew his own worth. He had all the big players in the boxing world after him. He had made his choice and in doing so signed a deal that was probably unheard of for a boxer at that time. It included a six-figure signing fee, use of a house, a Mercedes and living expenses of £500 per week. The boxing revenues were split 70 per cent for him and 30 per cent to the company, but that also covered training expenses, the salaries of the training team, health and life insurance policies and so on. It was a great package and my philosophy from day one was that I was working for him and that together we could both achieve things. I never got the 25 per cent cut many people thought I did, but I had no complaints. We both had the world at our feet and I knew we both wanted to be winners in what we were going to be doing.

Things weren't going so smoothly in my personal life with Jackie. We'd had lots of ups and downs by the time I became the manager of Lennox Lewis. Both she and I could be volatile and there were often explosions of temper. I don't think for one minute that I was the perfect husband and I now believe that we didn't really give ourselves a chance with the way we rushed into things. Jackie obviously didn't know anything about the thoughts I carried with me about wanting to be a female and feeling that I'd been born into the wrong body. Perhaps some of my behaviour was down to what I was trying to hide. It certainly couldn't have helped, even if I was never consciously aware of it causing a problem. By the time Lennox came along, there was a kind of uneasy peace that existed between Jackie and me. Throwing everything into my job probably didn't help matters, but the writing had been on the wall for quite a while when we split up in the summer of 1990. I moved out to a house we had not too far from The Crayford Arms while Jackie continued to run the pub with her new boyfriend.

Lennox's career was going along with far more success. He was gaining experience as a professional by fighting regularly and he was winning. At the end of October that year he became European heavyweight champion in only his 14th fight and that in turn led to the prospect of a huge contest with another unbeaten heavyweight, Gary Mason, who was much more experienced and held the British title. I should have been in high spirits as the year drew to a close but everything suddenly came tumbling down around me when the Levitt Group crashed. The company – thought to be worth around £150 million and supposed to be as solid as a rock – crumbled overnight.

Roger Levitt was the supreme salesman and a man who never lacked confidence. Even when there were police and liquidators roaming the offices of the Group, he was still telling me everything would be all right and sorted out. I was left with the feeling that everything was about to disappear.

I was devastated but determined to do all I could to make sure I rescued the situation. I spent a lot of time with the administrators who wanted to know all about Lennox's contract. I remained Lewis's manager under the terms of the British Board of Control agreement we had signed, and he was also signed to Frank Maloney Promotions and Management. I had to start talking to potential new backers as quickly as I could.

I made contact with various people on both sides of the Atlantic while knowing there would be plenty of people who would have loved to see me fail to rescue the situation and go under. The cost of trying to keep everything together at this time was a problem as I had no real income as Christmas approached and the situation was also taking its toll mentally. Emotionally, I was a mess and driving home from London one evening I actually contemplated suicide. It was only for a split second and I swerved to avoid the trees I'd thought about crashing into, but the idea had been there and it frightened me. Later in my life dark thoughts and depression would resurface to cause me to contemplate taking my own life due to my gender problems.

In the end it was a call from Roger Levitt that would eventually lead to someone else financing the operation. The two people I met through Levitt were a businessman called Conrad Morris and an accountant named Panos Eliades who specialised in liquidation cases. Panos was going to take on Roger's role while Conrad seemed keen to stay in the background and it was Panos who I would work alongside for the ten years that followed. For the first time in weeks I was able to feel more relaxed and I could feel some of the tension disappearing.

With a new deal in place I could continue in my role as Lennox's manager and within months he had won his fight with Mason, with Gary stopped in the seventh round and Lennox becoming extremely hot boxing property. I was determined to enjoy the victory and celebrated after the fight at a party in a friend's pub. I was in a really euphoric mood but that all changed a few days later when an envelope was stuffed through the letterbox in Crayford. It contained a bunch of keys and a short note from Jackie telling me she wasn't going to be running the pub anymore which she had as part of the agreement when we'd split up.

I hadn't really paid any attention to how it was doing or what was going on. I had Emma living with me in the house and I was simply working hard at building my boxing business.

I found out that the pub was in debt but with the help of my mum and her boyfriend, John, we managed to turn it around. I began to use the pub as a base and in the end things worked out pretty well when it could have been an absolute disaster. That episode really did signal the end for Jackie and me, and a few years later we were divorced. We had hurtled into our marriage and in the end I think our relationship suffered because of it. The one thing I know we both gained was having our beautiful daughter Emma and for that I will always be grateful.

In many ways the Mason fight was a taste of things to come. The win raised Lennox's profile and mine as well. I'd been known for a few years in the world of boxing and there were occasions when somebody might recognise me in the street, but on the whole I'd been pretty low key. The Mason fight began to change all that. But if that was big, then the one which took place 19 months down the line, against Donovan 'Razor' Ruddock at the end of October 1992, moved the Lewis operation into another league.

By this time there was a new woman in my life, and yes, she was small, blonde and pretty. I'd met her in Stringfellows night-club when I'd gone there with a friend called David Byrne, who had played for Millwall, and he'd brought along a few of his footballing mates. We were all drinking champagne and as usual I had no trouble portraying the image of a Jack-the-lad figure, out for a night of fun with some of the boys. I'd just come back from America where Lennox had beaten veteran former world champion Mike Weaver. I spotted a girl who really interested me and I watched her dancing with a friend before introducing myself. There was no doubt she was attractive and I could see a few of the other guys look at the two of us. Her name was Caroline, she'd been married to someone in Dubai and had a daughter from the relationship. We exchanged telephone numbers and it wasn't long before we were seeing a lot of each other.

There was no pressure on me to have a long-term relationship, but something in me obviously wanted that to happen. My feelings of wanting to be a woman hadn't gone away, but I was managing them. I was living for the moment. Because so much was going on and it was all so exciting, I just got caught up in the whole thing and began to enjoy the ride I was on. It was a terrific experience and one I would probably never have believed would be possible, but it certainly wasn't all fun and games. There was an awful lot of hard work involved and there was also a great deal of stress that went with it as well. It was a very steep learning curve as I had to get to grips with the complexities of doing boxing business at the very highest level of the sport. The upcoming fight with Ruddock was to be huge because the winner of the contest would then get to fight for the world heavyweight title. The money would be astronomical. Before Lennox met Ruddock I was in San Diego when I got a call from someone with an unmistakable voice. It was Don King.

'Frank Maloney, how are you, my little man?' he asked me.

I had met King a few times and knew he would have loved to have signed Lennox. The legendary promoter was used to getting what he wanted when it came to fights and fighters. He was relentless and during my time with Lewis I became used to King trying to wear me down to get the deal he wanted. On this occasion he was trying to get a piece of the promotional action when Lennox fought Ruddock. I didn't really have time to reply to his initial question before he launched into what turned out to be classic Don King.

'Maloney,' he said, 'I'm going to make sure you're the biggest name in boxing Britain has ever seen. People like me and you, we come from the same background. We're both from oppressed minorities. I'm black and you're Irish. They want to try and make sure they keep us down. They don't want us to succeed, but they can't stop us!' He followed this by talking at length about, among other things, the potato famine in Ireland. There was no stopping him and he was in full flow as he finally got towards the real reason he'd called. 'You're the man, you can help steer things my way,' he claimed. 'You're the man who can help do that and if it happens I can make you rich. How does $1 million sound to you?' I simply told him that my loyalties were to Lennox and Main Events, the American promotional company we worked with. It wouldn't be my last encounter with Don King.

The fight with Ruddock was an amazing event, with the publicity bigger than anything I'd been involved in before. The contest was staged at Earls Court in London and the place was absolutely rocking. I'd never seen anything like it. The atmosphere was electric and the noise was incredible. Lennox produced an amazing display to stop Ruddock in the second round. It was a brilliant performance that emphasised his class and punching power. It also meant that the chance of fighting for the world heavyweight title was edging closer.

CHAPTER TEN

Parallel lives

I was on a high following the win over Ruddock and I let the feeling of euphoria I was experiencing slip over into my private life. In the months leading up to the fight my relationship with Caroline had become strained. We had our flare-ups and she'd gone off to Dubai for a while. We got together again just before the fight and soon after it I bought Caroline an engagement ring and we set up home together in a Surbiton flat.

I don't know if it was the happiness and relief I felt at Lennox getting the win over Ruddock that triggered my decision. The victory certainly meant a lot to everyone connected with the Lewis camp. We had worked long and hard to make sure he got to the position he now found himself in and with a world title fight in the offing it seemed as though a whole new chapter had opened up for all of us. Whether I felt the need to make sure I maintained my normal life by setting up home with Caroline, I don't really know. Once again, if I had done the sensible thing, I would have given myself time to think things through and question whether I was doing the right thing, but I didn't. At the time I probably did think it was something that I wanted, but I suspect I was kidding myself. It really boiled down to the fact that I liked being in a relationship, but that it was really for the wrong reasons. The trappings of a guy in my position suited me. Nice home, nice car, money in my pocket and a pretty blonde on my arm – the Frank Maloney image was there for everyone to see. I made a lot of decisions without thinking too much about them. One thing seemed to lead to another and suddenly I had a public image. To a large extent I enjoyed it.

Having done such a good job in beating Ruddock, Lennox never actually got the chance to win the world title belt in the ring. Instead, he was awarded it at a ceremony one evening early in 1993 at a west London hotel when he should have gone on to fight either Evander Holyfield or Riddick Bowe. Evander was the world heavyweight champion under three of boxing's governing bodies – the WBC (World Boxing Council), WBA (World Boxing Association) and IBF (International Boxing Federation). He lost all three belts when he was beaten in a fight with Bowe and we had a real problem getting Bowe's camp to agree to the fight with Lewis. Eventually, Bowe relinquished the WBC version of the world title while keeping the other two and the WBC awarded the belt to Lennox. It was an unusual move, but at least Lewis was the champion and within months he was to earn a vast amount of money to defend his crown in a mandatory defence against a Don King boxer named Tony Tucker in Las Vegas.

King went into overdrive in negotiations for the percentage split of the purse money. He wanted 60–40 in Lennox's favour while we were looking for 80–20. In the end the WBC decided that it should be 75–25 in our favour. King had earned the right to stage the contest in Vegas through a sealed-purse bid and it turned out he had offered an astounding $12 million for the contest, meaning that Lennox would walk away with a cool $9 million for his first defence. Just four years earlier – in what was only his second professional fight – we had taken Lennox to Atlantic City in the USA to gain experience in a big promotion staged by King that featured world champion Mike Tyson in a title defence against Carl Williams. Lennox beat a boxer called Bruce Johnson in the second round and was paid $1,000.

Thanks to Don King my profile both in the UK and in the USA was raised to a new level, although I'm pretty sure that wasn't his intention judging by the prolonged and personal campaign he mounted against me in the build-up to the big day. Being involved at the sharp end of negotiations was an education and a test of my character, because a lot of what went on was designed to drive a wedge between Lennox and me. The first taste I got of King's insults was in London when we had a press conference to publicise the Vegas fight. He had a go at me and my management of Lewis in a speech that lasted for 73 minutes! It was pure King but I wasn't going to let it upset me. I knew what I was doing with Lennox and he would have let me know if he wasn't satisfied. I also knew that I still had other boxers who I was looking after. Only the night before I had felt dejected because another heavyweight of mine, Warren Richards, had lost on a show at York Hall. I loved the whole experience I was having with Lewis but I also loved boxing.

We did more press conferences in the USA and made a commercial for Showtime, the TV company that was screening the fight. They sent Concorde tickets for Lennox, me and my brother Eugene, who was acting as Lewis's personal security man. It was certainly different to anything else I'd done in boxing to publicise a show and it was an illustration of how things had changed since Lennox became world champion. Dan Duva was the man in charge at Main Events and I got on really well with him. He was a lawyer and not the normal sort of promoter you would expect, especially in the USA. He knew his way around big-time boxing and was a good teacher. He was always there with advice and wise words.

'Frank,' he told me, 'there are two sorts of business in this sport. There's boxing business and then there's heavyweight boxing business. Right now you're at the top of the heap because you manage the heavyweight champion of the world, so make sure you enjoy it and use it properly.' In other words he was telling me to use the power and status that came with being at the top. I could see what he meant – when you were in the position I was in, there would be an awful lot of people who would want to know me and be my friend. It gave me a certain position within the boxing hierarchy, but some people out there were also going to try and make sure my position in that hierarchy was short-lived.

We arrived in Las Vegas about ten days before the fight and the place was incredible. It was a whole new world for me and I loved it. The suite I had at the Mirage hotel was massive and the whole town had an air of excitement to it with everyone looking forward to the big day. In the week leading up to the fight King really started to turn up the pressure and also tried to make things personal. In doing so he only succeeded in making me famous. He called me a 'pugilistic pygmy' and a 'mental midget'. I was also a 'weasel', a 'snake in the grass' and 'treacherous'. He spotted my mother one day in the hotel and asked her how such a beautiful woman could have such a horrible son like me. It was non-stop. He even went to the trouble of having a letter printed and pushed under the doors of the journalists in town. Headed

Here I am dressed up as a cowboy (*top left*) and on the beach with my brothers Eugene and Vince with my father (*top right*). I was also the goalkeeper for St James FC (*bottom*).

I became interested in boxing from an early age and frequently went to the gym to practice (*top left*). I also met my first wife Jackie when I was fairly young and here we are on our wedding day, flanked by my parents (*bottom*). We had our first child, Emma, in 1976 (*top right*).

Jackie and I take Emma and our nephew Eugene to Cornwall for the day (*top*). Meanwhile, I get more involved in the boxing industry, becoming a coach and a manager (*bottom*).

Lennox and I catch up in my pub in Crayford in 1990.

Tracy and me are joined by Lennox for a photo at our wedding.

Lennox, Courtney Shand, baby Sophie and I pose for a photo in Lake Tahoe.

Me and my mum, Maureen.

Me and my wonderful daughters Sophie and Libby – on a flight to Australia with Libby (*left*) and with the two of them in Portugal (*bottom*).

I have an amazing family and I love them dearly. Here we all are in 2009: (*top, left to right*) Robyn, Emma, me, Sophie, and my grandchildren Libby and Ollie. And with my daughters Libby, Emma and Sophie in 2014.

Here I am with my daughter Emma in 1999 (*top*) and in 2014 (*left*).

'The indiscretions of Frank Maloney. Vicious, stupid or both?', the letter was addressed to Lennox, his family and genuine friends. It claimed Lewis was being held back by me.

King clearly wanted to try and undermine my position within the Lewis camp and maybe he thought he could intimidate me, but it didn't work. I stayed calm and acted as I always had done, which probably infuriated him even more. I got a lot of media attention because of Don and I just laughed the whole thing off. The UK press lapped it up and saw it for what it was, and as I never let things get to me and joked about King's comments, the US media also loved it. They couldn't believe that I wasn't going to take the bait and start shouting my mouth off at Don. I was determined to steer my way through all the nonsense and concentrate on the job in hand.

Mind you, it wasn't all work. One evening I went out and got a bit drunk with some of the press. I had gone out wearing cut-off dungarees and a cap turned backwards on my head but when I got back to the hotel the cap had been replaced with a condom as I stood at the bar chatting to an American woman. I was told later that someone had asked who I was. When they were told I was the manager of the world heavyweight champion, they couldn't quite believe it! I suppose it was the sort of thing that added to the whole Frank Maloney image, but it wasn't something that I played for effect. I was just being me and trying to unwind during a week in which I'd been working around the clock.

On the morning of the fight I was my usual nervous self. It was always like that. It wasn't through a lack of confidence, but I always managed to control those nerves and make sure I got on with what had to be done. In the dressing room before a fight it was always important to have a very calm and professional approach. In the fight, Lennox knocked Tucker down a couple of times, and showed what a good boxer he was, ending the fight with a points win to retain his title. It was a sweet victory for everyone involved and it set up what was to be a massive all-British affair with a defence against Frank Bruno. This fight was to have a profound effect on me – not because of what happened in the ring, but in my private life.

My relationship with Caroline leading up to the Bruno fight had not been good. She had become increasingly irritated by the time I spent travelling and working. The contest was to be held in the open air at Cardiff Arms Park in Wales on a Friday night at the beginning of October 1993 and the whole Lewis team had gone to Cardiff a couple of weeks before the fight. We practically took over the International hotel in the city. The place was busy all the time with a lot of the local young women very keen to get to know some of the sparring partners who we'd brought with us from the USA. Caroline went to Spain to stay at a villa owned by a friend of mine. I thought it was a good move because of the way things were between us. It meant she could have a break in the sun and then fly back to see the fight while I was able to get on with my job without getting into arguments with her.

The more I thought about my relationship with Caroline, the more I realised that it was on its last legs. I wondered why I had ever got involved in the first place. There had been times when the desire to be a female came back with a vengeance. On one occasion I'd been chatting to a girl in a hotel in London. She didn't know who I was but after a few drinks she was happy to go upstairs to her room and we ended up swapping clothes. She must have thought it was some sort of sex game but it was purely because I wanted to feel like a woman. And when I was away at training camps in the USA I had time to think while I was alone in my room at night and that's when the female side of my character would occupy my mind. I knew I had to continue being Frank, because I had gone too far down the road to let anything spoil things now. I had too much to lose although I wasn't trying to delude myself that my female side might one day go away.

In the build-up to the Bruno fight, one of Lennox's training camps had been in Washington and one night we got an invitation to go to Lorton state penitentiary to watch bouts between some of the inmates. It might not seem like the ideal night out to most people but we were all grateful for the distraction and it turned out to be a real eye-opener. There were prisoners in there doing life sentences that meant they were never going to come out and some of them arrived for their bouts chained hand and foot. Lennox was given a big reception and it was clear they were pleased to see us. For me, it wasn't just about the boxing. Some of the inmates who were watching the bouts were known as the prison 'bitches'. They were 'shemales' and some of them had breasts. I sat there fascinated by what I saw and I couldn't help noticing the way they were brushing their hair and putting on lipstick. I managed to talk to one of them and it was quite sad to hear the way some had opted to be the way they were simply to survive the prison system. I wondered if any of them had the inner thoughts and feelings I had, whether they had always wanted to be female and through a freak of birth found themselves born with the wrong body. But there was no way I was going to start having that sort of conversation with them.

By the time I arrived in Cardiff I think I'd already made up my mind to end things with Caroline. I started to believe that perhaps I'd gone into the relationship partly as a way of making sure I didn't go down the route of transitioning. I would wake up each morning and my outward appearance would always be of someone who was happy, someone who was in control.

There were lots of times when I wished I didn't have to put on an act, but it was as if each day I put on a suit and this suit was Frank Maloney. I got dressed in it and I went off and became the character everyone expected me to be. I was comfortable being Frank, especially when I was working, but in the quiet moments I would reflect and think, why am I doing this?

I decided to make sure I didn't get involved with anyone again. There was a part of me that wanted to be Frank Maloney and that part of my personality was always fighting my inner self, the part that I was trying to keep a lid on. I was so frightened to let that side of me get out and sometimes it became very difficult for me. I'd feel down and get depressed and although I never allowed myself to be seen like that in public, the female part of me was always banging on the door, trying to get out. It could happen at different times and situations. Sometimes I'd be sitting on a plane flying over the Atlantic and my mind would drift away with thoughts about wanting to be female. I'd often read women's magazines when I went on trips and I started finding out more about the world of transsexuals. But I was still determined to keep a lid on it. I felt that if I gave in just a little and started dressing in women's clothes, I would never be able to stop. That the female side of my character would have been let loose and I would not be able to rein it back in. If that happened I knew I would lose so much.

Being in a relationship with Caroline helped stave things off and a part of me, the Frank part, genuinely liked women and was happy not just to flirt with them but also to talk and enjoy their company. But by the time I got to Cardiff and was in the middle of all the preparations for the big fight, the last thing I wanted was a long-term relationship. At least that was how I felt as I sat alone one morning in the reception area of the hotel. I must have looked pretty depressed because one of the waitresses came over and asked me what was wrong.

'I'm bored,' I told her.

She must have thought I was mad, because there I was at the centre of everything that was going on. There was no shortage of female company if I'd wanted it, but most of the girls who were in and out of the hotel were not the sort of women I was going to sit down and talk to. It wasn't as if I was looking to whisk anyone off to my bedroom, I just felt the need to chat to a nice girl. I told the waitress this and she said she had an air hostess friend who might be just the sort of girl I was talking about. A couple of days later I noticed two good-looking girls in the hotel reception area, one blonde and the other brunette. The waitress introduced us. The blonde was the girl I'd been told about, Tracey Lewis.

We went out for a meal and then back to my hotel where we chatted for quite some time. She was really easy to talk to and I felt comfortable and relaxed being with her. I wasn't looking for a relationship but I did find Tracey attractive. She was very good looking, small and blonde, but it was her personality that I really warmed to and we decided to go for a drink the next night. I found her very easy to get along with and I wanted to be up front about what had been going on in my life with regard to Caroline, that the relationship was on its last legs but I hadn't actually finished things with her.

Caroline herself flew in from Spain for the fight which Lennox won, stopping Frank in the seventh round. The next day Caroline and I had a blazing row and she clearly wasn't happy with the way things were going between us. It really signalled the end. I moved into a hotel for a few weeks, and then we split up for good. It was inevitable really and it seemed more apparent than ever to me that I needed some time and space on my own.

I did see Tracey a few times and she also came to London and met my family. They all liked her and she got on well with them. It was clear from their reaction that they thought she was the right sort of girl for me, but I let things drift. I'm sure there must have been a bit of a conflict in my brain. I knew that I shouldn't get mixed up with another girl in a serious relationship, but at the same time I liked her. I couldn't tell anyone at all the real reason why I thought it was wrong to get into anything long-term. The trouble was, I don't think I really admitted it to myself at the time, even though I knew that was the truth.

Eugene liked Tracey as well and it was through him that we started seeing each other once more. It was easy for me to pick up where I'd left off. Our relationship gradually grew and we just seemed to get on so well. There was no pressure from her. She didn't want or ask for anything from me. I just felt very comfortable being with her, but I was also aware that my feminine feelings, far from lessening or disappearing, were actually getting stronger.

I had by now moved back into my mum's council flat in the East End of London and although I was the manager of the heavyweight champion of the world you would hardly have thought it from my lifestyle. There was no big house in the country or exotic holidays, but I had never needed material things. My mum's flat was convenient because a lot of my work was in London and I was happy. I remember getting back once having stopped off at the local fish and chip shop to find a phone message from Donald Trump. I couldn't help thinking that he was probably sitting in a plush office in the USA and there I was in my mum's little flat tucking into a nice bit of cod.

I had some women's clothes hidden away at the flat to satisfy the part of me that was more curious than ever to explore my feminine feelings. I would also get magazines sent to me and in one I saw an advert that captured my imagination. It simply urged, 'Be the girl you've always dreamed of being,' for anyone who wanted to know how to dress and act like a woman. I wanted to know more, to explore what had always gone on in my head. This was a service that offered me the chance to explore and perhaps gain a better understanding of those inner feelings.

I phoned the number in the magazine and a woman answered. She was the person who taught clients how to act and behave as a girl and I told her that I was little bit wary of using the service simply because I was quite well known. She assured me that wouldn't be a problem as her customers included judges and MPs. The one thing she was very strict about was not tolerating lateness or any undignified behaviour. 'I teach all of my girls to be young ladies,' she insisted.

I had to send a deposit of £5 to a post office box and once she'd received my postal order she called me back on a mobile phone I had specially got for the purpose. I was desperate to make sure I didn't get caught. I knew there was a danger that something might go wrong and I would be exposed, but there was also something inside me that drove me on.

When the day came, I got up in the morning determined to go through with the appointment. I shaved my legs in preparation and got in my car to drive to the location she'd given me near Hampstead. But on the way I just froze. I suddenly thought that if I went through with it I'd be admitting that I had a problem or, more to the point, I had a problem that I wasn't able to control. I turned the car around and headed back home. For the rest of the day I was in a foul mood, partly because I was caught in the battle that was raging between the two sides of my personality and also because I hadn't really been strong enough to go through with the appointment. I phoned the woman and apologised, saying something had come up, but she was firm with me on the phone.

'I don't really accept what you've just said,' she told me.

I think she knew that when it came to the crunch I had lost my nerve and I suspect it had happened with other potential clients. She gave me another date, but I didn't go. If I'm honest, I was just too frightened of being exposed. I'd been all over the media because of my work and I believed there was a real chance that I would be recognised. Once again I would get back to being Frank Maloney.

Tracey visited me in London more often now and I would spend time in Cardiff. Part of me felt that if I wasn't on my own so much, I could keep my feminine side under control. I was attracted to Tracey and it was genuine. When I was with Tracey I was Frank, I wasn't thinking about being a woman or the feminine side of my character. At one point I got rid of all my women's clothes because I was starting to feel more serious about Tracey and I felt guilty – by having this secret and hiding the clothes I was betraying my relationship with her. What we had together was growing stronger every time I saw her.

I'd made up my mind that I wasn't going to get into anything serious with another woman, but I found myself getting closer to Tracey. She wasn't like any other girl I'd met before and we didn't rush things. We had a friendship very early on and, as that grew, my love for her grew too. She was quiet, reserved and really didn't crave the high life. She was happy to give me the time and space to get on with my job, realising how important it was to me and I never felt under pressure with her. In the end our relationship blossomed without either of us really noticing it and suddenly we were a couple. I felt that I'd met someone who I had fallen in love with, who I could one day marry and who I could see out my life with. My determination to make sure things worked with her also kept my feminine side at bay. I didn't have to play the macho man with her.

In the summer of 1994 I was in the Catskills in the USA as Lennox prepared in his training camp for a forthcoming title defence in London when I got a call from Tracey. She told me she was pregnant. In less than a year I'd gone from thinking I should never have a relationship again to becoming a father at the age of 41. The following March I stood with tears in my eyes feeling emotional as Tracey gave birth to Sophie. Being at the birth of your child is incredible for any father and I suppose I must have seemed like any other proud dad, but it obviously meant more to me to know that I had become a father again. Had I been selfish by going ahead with my relationship with Tracey? I don't think so as I didn't do it simply to maintain a normal life. Yet, however well things worked, perhaps there was an inevitability about what would happen further down the line.

CHAPTER ELEVEN

Driving force

In September 1994 my professional life was turned upside down when Lennox Lewis unexpectedly lost his world heavyweight title against American boxer Oliver McCall at Wembley Arena. It was a routine defence that should not have troubled Lennox, but heavyweight boxing often throws up shocks – if guys that size connect with one good punch they can take out their opponent. Lennox was sent to the floor in the second round and, although he somehow managed to get to his feet again, he was stopped by the referee.

At ringside I was hit by a wave of emotion which quickly turned to anger as I made my feelings known to WBC boss José Sulaimán. I claimed the referee had stopped the fight too soon and photographers captured me on the spot with my face contorted into a picture of pure anger and hate. It wasn't a great look, but I was in a state of shock. Everything we'd worked so hard to achieve as a team had been shattered in a split second by the fist of McCall. We'd even had a possible £12 million fight against Riddick Bowe lined up but there was no chance of that now. I left Wembley with Tracey and the tears began to stream down my face. I was numb and we walked together for about two miles before being stopped by a guy who offered us a lift to our hotel.

Having Tracey by my side certainly helped – we'd grown very close. I soon became extremely focussed on making sure we got Lennox into a position to win his title back. By the time Sophie was born six months later, Lewis was training in the USA for his first contest since losing. The bout was against Lionel Butler in California in May 1995 and Lennox got back to his winning ways with a fifth-round victory, but it would take a lot of hard work and tough bargaining before he would get the chance to fight for the title again. Top-level professional boxing is not just about two fighters getting in the ring – there is an awful lot of politics involved as well and in our case we even went to court to get what we felt we deserved.

Working your way up to the top of the tree after a fall can be a torturous business and there are so many obstacles in your way as you start that climb. McCall duly paid a return visit to London about a year after he had beaten Lennox. This time it was to defend the WBC title against Frank Bruno and this time it was Frank's turn to claim the glory when he became a world champion after three failed attempts. The win complicated things further for us, because Bruno's most likely opponent in his next fight was Mike Tyson.

Towards the end of the year the WBC held its convention in Thailand, providing a chance for fighters, managers and promoters to lobby for their side. There was always a lot of talking and deals struck at conventions because you had all the big players under one roof. I did my best to make sure Lennox would be

Bruno's next opponent rather than Tyson but it proved to be a hopeless task as a fight between Frank and Tyson was sanctioned by a 28–0 vote. But if the long journey to Thailand was a fruitless one in terms of boxing, I'd also decided to make a trip to Bangkok to find out more about something which had fascinated me since I was young.

As surprising as it may seem, I first heard the term 'ladyboy' from a friend of my dad. I was very young at the time and his Irish friend was in the merchant navy. He was talking all about his trips to Thailand and how he and his mates had met these ladyboys and been drinking with them. He told my dad how you couldn't tell the difference between them and real women. My dad didn't sound convinced and he said he could never have gone out drinking with them. His reaction was something I often thought about as I got older and it confirmed that he could never have accepted his own son telling him he wanted to be a woman. At the time I managed to sneak a look at some pictures this guy had taken and I was absolutely amazed at how beautiful the ladyboys were.

By the age of 42 I'd learned that there would be times when the Frank side of my character was going to have to give way and Thailand was one of them. I'd gone to the convention, was my usual Frank Maloney self and done my job. I'd been totally focussed on the work and the business. Once that was over I could so easily have just flown back to London, but I hopped on a plane to Bangkok to satisfy my curiosity and to feed the thoughts and feelings of the person I probably really should have been.

It was pretty easy to find a Bangkok bar that was full of ladyboys. I started talking to one after finding myself staring at her. 'I am a woman,' she said, and with that she took my hand and ran it across her throat just to let me feel that there was no Adam's apple. I knew from what I'd read that having one was a giveaway in those who only dressed as a woman. I took her back to my hotel room because I was fascinated and wanted to know more. She told me she had been born a boy but wanted to be a girl and I explained that was really what I wanted, that I was the same as her. We got on really well and she even suggested that the next time I was in Thailand I could stay with her. She offered to help me dress as a woman and to do my make-up. I explained that I couldn't really do that and said that I had a father back in England who would go mad at the thought of it – and I truly believed that.

I chatted to my new friend for about three hours and she was happy to tell me about the existence she led. She was on hormones and was working in the club as a hostess to fund the operation to fully transition. Her ambition was to someday marry a man and live as his wife. She seemed very comfortable with who she was. I couldn't help feeling she was lucky. At least she was being herself and there was I constantly fighting myself and thinking that I would never be able to go down the same route.

Before she left she scribbled down her name and address but when she'd gone I immediately screwed it up and threw it away. I knew that keeping it could open a can of worms for me and it could affect my relationship with Tracey. I suppose I felt a sense of guilt. I loved Tracey and we now had little Sophie to think about too. I was a lot more knowledgeable about the way I felt and the reason for it, and I still believed I could keep it under control. Trips to things like the convention and travelling a lot were part of my job. So too were long weeks spent in training camps. I was usually busy during the day though at night there was plenty of time for me to read magazines and explore my curiosity using the internet after I bought myself a laptop on one of my visits to the USA. But back in England my curiosity almost got me discovered by Panos.

He was meticulous when it came to money. He had sourced a central billing system for our phone lines and reasoned that it should include my home phone which I used a lot for business calls. The bills went straight to him and one morning I was in my office when he called.

'Frank, come and see me. I've got something to show you and you'll never believe it,' he told me. He showed me a list of numbers and the charges lined up against them. 'Guess what?' he asked. 'These are all sex lines! I've checked them out and you won't believe what some of them are about. It must be some pervert here who's making the calls. Listen to what they're saying.'

He dialled one of the numbers and I immediately recognised the voice. I suddenly realised that I had used the number. They weren't exactly sex lines – they were advertised for transgender people and for cross-dressing. I'd totally forgotten that I was on this centrally billed system and I'd made these calls from my home one day. I suppose because they were premium lines they must have stood out like a sore thumb. Luckily there was no number linked to the calls, but he was determined to get to the bottom of it and find out who had been making them. I knew it was only a matter of time before he discovered it was me. I had to do something to give myself time to come up with an excuse so I asked him if I could take a look at the sheet.

'Do you know what?' I asked him after a long pause. 'I bet they're from my home phone.'

'Yours!' said Panos looking totally amazed. 'But you wouldn't phone lines like that, would you?'

'No, no,' I insisted. 'Of course I wouldn't, but I bet it happened when Tracey had a few of her cabin crew around. A couple of the guys are gay and I remember getting home one evening when they'd all had a bit of wine and they were giggling and listening to stuff on the phone.'

I told Panos that I'd got annoyed with them and asked them to go. He seemed relieved to get an explanation and I was certainly relieved that he believed the story I'd just made up. Of course it had been a stupid thing to do and I should have been more careful, but the trouble was I always wanted to know more about the subject of transsexuals and transgender people. I devoured anything I could get my hands on. Some of it was informative and useful, other things were really only out there for sexual titillation. I once went to a newsagents near Times Square in New York that sold all sorts of publications and I found a magazine that had stories about transsexuals. I made a point of reading a copy every time I went to New York.

Although it had been difficult trying to get Lennox into a position to challenge for the world title again, he kept winning his fights. He put together four victories in a row before finally getting the chance to avenge his defeat against McCall and the two met for the vacant WBC crown in February 1997 at the Las Vegas Hilton. Lennox won the contest in strange circumstances as the American seemed to suffer something of a breakdown in the ring before the referee stopped the bout in the fifth round. Seeing McCall in tears and unwilling to fight wasn't pleasant and it was clear he had mental issues and should never have entered the ring. However, boxing is an unforgiving sport and although it might not have been the sort of victory we expected, the bottom line was that Lennox had got his title back and I was once more the manager of the heavyweight champion of the world. When he'd lost to McCall at Wembley, Dan Duva told me, 'The only thing better in boxing than winning the world heavyweight title is regaining it.' He was right.

It felt good to be in that position again after the upset following the loss to McCall. Lennox had worked hard to make sure he was in a position to regain the title and so had all of his team. It was a nice feeling for everyone involved and it was a special moment for me. Five months later, following a successful first defence of the title, I enjoyed another special moment – but this time it was very much to do with my personal life.

The defence was in July in Lake Tahoe in the USA against a British fighter named Henry Akinwande and although Lennox did a professional job the bout itself was hardly a classic because of the challenger's negative tactics. He was disqualified in the fifth round having spent most of the fight trying to hold and wrestle the champion.

The day after the win I'd arranged for Tracey and I to be married in the wedding chapel at Caesar's hotel. We'd talked about getting married for some time, but didn't want a huge affair in England. Lake Tahoe seemed perfect and I was genuinely happy to be getting married to her. I loved Tracey. We had liked each other from the start, we had grown together as people and we had fallen in love with each other. On the face of it there was no reason why the two of us shouldn't spend the rest of our lives together, except I knew that could never really be the case, not if I was being honest with myself.

Tracey was completely unaware that she was marrying someone with a secret. A secret I felt I would never be able to share with her. For some time after meeting Tracey I had managed to keep the feminine side of my character under lock and key. I felt the urges I had within me could ultimately destroy my life, the lives of the people closest to me and also everything I had worked so hard to achieve in my career. My need to explore the other side of my character would become stronger and more difficult to control. I had lived a double life for a long time, trying to deal with and manage the contrasting sides of my personality.

Continuing to do that would prove to be so much harder as the years went on. It's easy to look back now and say that I should never have got married for a second time. I had no idea of the torture and agony I would put Tracey through or the mental turmoil I would have to deal with.

We did manage a honeymoon in Venice but it was cut short after three days because I had to fly to New York to put Lennox's next defence in place. As usual Tracey, didn't complain. She knew that was part of our lives and understood how important it was to me and for us as a family. I couldn't have been married to someone who was more understanding when it came to my work.

The fact that she was so supportive and always there for me only made matters worse when I thought about how I would never be able to be absolutely honest with her. There was always stress involved with my job and often I would not be the easiest person to live with. I'd have moments where I could be in the same room as Tracey but be miles away, wrapped up in my own thoughts. I'm sure she assumed it was all work related and some of it was, but there was also my gender problem which would also contribute to those moments.

All of this was in no way a distraction when it came to acting professionally and making sure we remained on course for what would be a career-defining moment for Lewis, namely setting up a fight with Evander Holyfield for the undisputed heavyweight championship of the world. The fight did finally happen, in March 1999 at Madison Square Garden in New York, but the wheeling and dealing which took place in order to actually get to that point began more than a year before the contest took place.

By the time it happened I didn't have quite the same enthusiasm for the job. That didn't mean I was doing it badly. I threw myself at it just as I always had done and as usual I spent time at the training camp we'd set up in the Poconos. My routine followed what had become a familiar pattern. While I was busy and getting on with the job I was my usual Frank Maloney self, but whenever I was alone in my room I would sit for hours looking at different transgender sites on my laptop. I wanted to compare my own thoughts and feelings with those of other people who seemed to be very much like me. People who had stories to tell about their own lives and how they had coped with the problem I had. And yes, I did see it as a problem.

The Lewis–Holyfield contest was massive and even I perhaps didn't realise just how big it was until I got to New York in the final week before the fight. I couldn't help but be excited by the occasion and as well as Lennox getting his chance to become undisputed champion, by adding WBA and IBF titles to the WBC one he already held, it gave me the chance to claim my own bit of boxing history as his manager. I had been involved in boxing for 35 years and the sport meant a lot to me. Being part of its history would be a special moment for me and I was looking forward to it. However, what I didn't realise when I arrived in New York was that I would also experience one of the most stressful and emotional 48-hour periods of my entire life.

I had always loved the city and enjoyed my trips. I wanted to enjoy this one too, but I can't honestly say it was the best time I'd had in New York for a number of different reasons. As usual in the build-up to a big fight there was a tremendous buzz and excitement surrounding the contest, and those final few days before it actually took place were manic. We stayed in the New York Palace hotel and I had Tracey and little Sophie with me, although it wasn't as if I could spend that much time with them because there was always something that had to be done.

The bigger the fight, the greater the pressure and that week I certainly began to feel it. It was non-stop. I was used to the big fight scene, but I think being so close to realising the dream we'd all worked so hard for made this particular contest extra-special. Daily press conferences were always part of the build-up and I was aware of the important part the media played. I had a good relationship with the press, even though I'd had my run-ins with some of them, but it was never personal. I recognised that they had a job to do just the same as I did.

On the Thursday evening before the fight I'd arranged to take some of the journalists to a steak restaurant called Maloney and Porcelli in midtown Manhattan. The big group also included Don King, who I knew would keep everyone amused and could literally talk all night. There would be plenty of drinking going on as well as eating and I realised it wouldn't be difficult for me to slip out. Nobody was likely to notice and if they did it would be easy to make the excuse of wanting to get some fresh air and have a walk. I used to love walking the streets of New York and with the sort of week I'd had, no one could blame me for wanting a bit of free time on my own. But when I did slip away from the restaurant that night I headed for the Staten Island Ferry.

The magazine I'd discovered in the newsagents in Times Square contained a lot of adverts and on a previous visit one of them in particular had caught my eye. I think it was aimed not just at transsexuals but also transvestites and men who liked to cross-dress. You could go to this particular place and basically dress as a female and have your make-up done. The location was a house which was set up like a small hotel on Staten Island and was run by a couple of gay guys, one of whom was a professional make-up artist who worked in the theatre. On a previous visit I went there to get dressed in female clothes, had make-up put on and then just sat drinking coffee and chatting to some of the other people who were there. Nobody knew who I was and I said I was a salesman over from England on business. It was all very relaxing for the couple of hours I was there and then I went to a room, took the clothes and make-up off and left.

By the time I walked out of the restaurant in Manhattan that night I was ready to pay a return visit. I felt more stressed with every day that passed. I probably had more going on in my head than just the preparations for the fight. My inner thoughts and feelings hadn't disappeared and, if anything, I think they were perhaps becoming stronger. I had earlier got the number from the magazine as I had done before, made a phone call and was told that they were going to have a small party on Thursday night.

'You're welcome to come along to it if you'd like to,' the guy told me. 'There'll be other girls here, we serve wine and have some food and sometimes there are guys who come along who like T girls.'

When I ended the call my head was spinning. Should I go? What if I got caught? It would be just two days away from the biggest fight I'd ever been involved in. I knew it was crazy, but I felt that allowing my feminine side to take control, even if it was just for a few hours, would help ease the stress which had been building.

I got the ferry times and worked out exactly when I should leave the steak house. It was just as I thought it would be, I spent some time chatting to various people and then slipped away, got a taxi to where the ferry departed to Staten Island and then made my way to the house. I was nervous but knew I wanted to go through with the evening.

The same guy welcomed me and showed me to a room where I chose the clothes I wanted to wear and got dressed, and then sat in a chair while he put my make-up on. He started chatting to me about all the famous people he'd worked with as a make-up artist in the theatre and then went on to tell me that apart from the service I was receiving, which involved me paying a flat fee of around $30 to sit around dressed as a woman and have him do my make-up, there was also another option if I wanted to take it. I started to wonder whether he was going to suggest some sort of funny business, but it turned out to be nothing of the sort.

'You can come and stay here free of charge if you want to,' he told me. 'We offer a service where you actually work as chambermaid, cleaning the rooms in the morning, but then you have the rest of the day to yourself before helping to serve some of the customers in the evening. It means we save on the cost of having to employ staff and it also means you get to stay dressed throughout the day.'

I thought I've got the heavyweight champion of the world fighting in less than 48 hours and he's just asked me if I want to be a chambermaid! I politely declined and went upstairs to where he said there were drinks and food. I went in expecting a room full of people but I was alone. I sat around for about 45 minutes and the guy was very apologetic, saying I was early and that most of the people would be arriving later.

I began to think about what was going on and started to ask myself, what am I doing here?. Why am I putting myself at risk in this fashion? If something were to happen to me, how on earth would I explain what I was doing in a place like this? The thoughts suddenly began to frighten me and it was as if I came to my senses within seconds. I'd desperately needed to dress as a female. To look and feel like a woman and, even though it had been for a short period, it did make me feel better, but then the reality of my situation struck home with a vengeance. It was as if Frank had burst into the room and taken control and told my female side to get lost. I explained to the owner that I had to go and he tried to tell me things would liven up in a couple of hours, but my mind was made up. I quickly got changed, scrubbed the make-up off my face and took a taxi back to the ferry terminal.

I'd probably been gone for no more than a couple of hours and thankfully nobody queried my explanation when I got back to the restaurant, not even Tracey, who had come along for the evening with a couple of friends of ours. Tracey knew that in the week leading up to big fights I got stressed and she would always leave me alone to do what I wanted. Telling everyone that I'd been walking around New York in order to get rid of some of the stress I was feeling seemed a perfectly logical explanation to them. I even suggested to our friends that the four of us should go out to a club and that's exactly what we did. Once again, the public face of Frank Maloney was on show to the world just hours after I had been sitting in a room on Staten Island dressed as a woman and calling myself Linda.

There was no doubt I seemed to be getting more reckless. What I did that night in Staten Island could have destroyed my world. It was as if I was pushing the boundaries I'd set myself, just to see how far I could go. The more I fought against those feelings, the stronger they seemed to be when they came back and, to be honest, it began to frighten me. I really didn't want to be different, but knew I was. I wanted to have a normal and happy marriage to Tracey and I loved little Sophie with all my heart, but sometimes I felt as though my head was going to explode with all that was going on. I'd pray at night and when I did, part of me was asking to be a girl and the other part was asking God to help me beat what I felt was wrong with me. I asked for the strength to make sure those inner feelings didn't take over my life. I still felt that my personality was split between the Frank Maloney everyone knew and my feminine self. The trouble was, I began to feel the Frank side of my character was getting weaker.

I used to set myself goals throughout my career and once I'd achieved those goals I'd wonder what I could do next. Making that piece of boxing history with Lennox becoming the undisputed champion was my next goal and as the fight edged closer I had no doubt in my mind that he would beat Holyfield. In many ways I didn't think it could get any better or any bigger. I had actually thought about the possibility of walking away after the fight because I'd achieved everything I'd set out to do ten years earlier and I wondered if it could only go downhill from this point. But what was to happen in Madison Square Garden changed any thoughts I had of taking that particular route and once again it was the public face of Frank Maloney that came to the fore when the verdict was announced in the ring after 12 rounds of boxing.

Unbelievably, the fight ended in a draw and, not surprisingly, this verdict caused uproar. I thought Lennox had clearly won it and virtually everyone else at the fight that night did too. I instinctively started ranting and raving about the injustice of it all and in classic Frank fashion I claimed that even Stevie Wonder could have seen that Lennox won it. I felt an emotional wreck – it wasn't just the fight which had taken its toll on me, but it was also the turmoil I'd had to deal with on the morning of the contest.

Things hadn't exactly been going smoothly with Panos for some time, but I still wasn't prepared to be told on the phone by a reporter that he'd heard from his office in London that I'd been sacked. He claimed that Panos had said something on a pre-recorded television programme which had been shown back in Britain the night before.

'He's basically said that you're out as of today,' he informed me.

I was absolutely stunned and also very hurt. I'd worked so hard and been loyal to Panos and the company. Now, on the morning of the biggest fight I'd ever been involved in, I was being told that he wanted me out of the picture. The shock and hurt soon gave way to pure anger. I couldn't get him on the phone so I went straight to his room in the hotel and confronted him. He claimed to be mystified by the whole thing, even when I showed him a copy of the story which was being run in the UK. I knew he'd said what he'd said, but when he was finally persuaded to give an interview to the British media in the hotel lobby, he said that I wasn't going to be sacked and still seemed puzzled by the whole thing. It certainly wasn't what I needed on a day when my insides would be churning with anxiety. That whole 48-hour period was incredible and I think if I'd been wearing some kind of heart monitor it would probably have exploded.

The aftermath of the fight was amazing. The verdict not only made the back pages, there were headlines on the front of all the New York papers screaming that Lennox had been robbed of the victory his performance deserved. I gave endless interviews to anyone who wanted to talk to me about the fight and my face was all over the newspapers and television. I didn't give it a thought at the time, but I have since wondered if the guy in Staten Island ever saw any of the publicity that surrounded the fight and whether he realised that the girl he'd been chatting to as we waited for the other guests to arrive, was in fact manager of the world heavyweight champion.

CHAPTER TWELVE

Help

Everyone connected with the Lewis camp was bitterly disappointed at what had happened, but one man who still had a smile on his face after the fight was Don King, because he was already talking about a re-match and that meant him being involved in another mega-promotion. I had shouted and screamed about how ridiculous I thought the verdict had been. It wasn't planned as a strategy, but a couple of the press guys told me later that they felt the injustice we'd suffered would have been swept under the carpet had I not made such a fuss. I began to think that perhaps the whole thing had happened for a reason and maybe I was meant to stay in boxing despite the doubts I'd been experiencing. Having got so close to realising the dream, there was no way I was going to walk away from everything, especially as I was more convinced than ever that any re-match would see Lennox winning.

It took another eight months before a second meeting with Holyfield happened and the return confrontation was staged in Las Vegas. By the time it came around I had begun to feel more like an outsider within the Lewis camp. My relationship with Panos was still not good and my instinctive feeling in the months that led up to the contest was that things just didn't seem the same anymore, which was sad. I wondered if perhaps after ten years the whole thing was coming to a natural end for me, but I was determined to do my job as well as I'd ever done it and when I got to Vegas I began to get a bit of my old spark back. The build-up to the fight and excitement it generated was infectious. It gave me a lift to be at the centre of everything and I wanted to enjoy the moment and the win I was convinced Lennox would get.

I do now wonder just how my mood was affected at this time by the continuing conflict going on inside me. It wasn't as if I had a word with myself to make sure the front I was putting on as Frank Maloney didn't slip. It became an automatic part of my life but I also think it was taking an increasing toll and played a part in my mood when I wasn't showing my public face.

Tracey and Sophie were in Vegas with me for the fight. Tracey always seemed to understand that quite often I might not be in a particularly great frame of mind. She had no way of knowing what was going on in my head. If I had to put on an act in my public life, then the one I kept up in my private life was probably even greater. It was very difficult lying silently in bed beside the woman you loved knowing that no matter how much you thought of her and how much you cared for her, there was always going to be something you could never tell her. She had no idea that when I closed my eyes at night I would sometimes do so with tears rolling down my cheeks. For more than six years I had concealed my secret from her, not just to protect myself, but also to protect our marriage.

I was my usual nervous self as the fight grew nearer. I'd have probably got worried if I'd not been nervous. It was all part of the routine and as horrible as it was, it meant that I still cared about what I did. The contest went the distance and there was the usual wait before the scores were read out. I knew Lennox had won, but then I knew he'd won the first contest and look at what happened. Eventually the scores came through from the judges and this time there was no disputing the verdict as all three of them gave the contest to Lewis. After all the months and years of hard work and dreams, this was the night when it had finally fallen into place and Lennox was the undisputed heavyweight champion of the world. It sounded good and it felt good for everyone in his team. As for me, I finally had my little piece of boxing history, but the overriding emotion I felt that evening was one of relief. Having been so close eight months earlier only to be robbed of the victory, I was desperate to make sure that nothing like that happened again.

I was totally drained after the fight but showed my face at a celebration party before accepting an invitation from one of the many Lennox fans who asked me if I wanted to go to one of the local pubs on the strip. He was really surprised when I said, 'Yes', but I enjoyed mixing with the regular fans who had spent their money to come over and support us. I wasn't there for too long, because I was so tired and in a bit of a daze. I wanted to get back to my hotel and be with Tracey. It was a great moment for both of us. I'd achieved my dream and she had been a big part of making it come true.

It would have been lovely to have been able to just sit with her that night and open up. Tell her exactly what was going on with me, explain the torment I was going through and ask for her help and understanding, but I knew that could not happen. I still felt

I could just carry on as I always had. Living from day to day and filling those days up as best I could. But I couldn't help feeling that I'd cheated on Tracey in the way in which I was living two lives.

In the lead-up to the Holyfield fight I had once again spent quite a bit of time in the training camp in the Poconos, which meant downtime on the internet looking up transsexual sites. I was getting a lot of information, but in a strange way it just made matters worse. I would read an article and wonder if I was perhaps a transvestite, but then I'd ask myself why I had the desires I had to be a woman. I also spent a lot of time on different transsexual phone lines. I usually bought phone cards with preloaded credit that were useful because any number I called was untraceable as it wasn't a direct call.

There was also the store just down the road from the Poconos training camp which sold all kinds of sex magazines. I might leave some of the normal lads' mags around in my room, which did no harm at all to my reputation, but the ones I was really interested in, the ones about transgender and transsexuals, I would hide away. I became a master of deceit, but I also put myself at risk with my burning desire to discover more.

Back in England I discovered a company which specialised in clothes and merchandise for transsexuals. You could go there and spend some time dressed and talk to people who knew all about the subject. They had a branch in Dublin and for some reason I felt it would be safer for me to go to Dublin because I wouldn't be recognised, which was crazy really. I was pretty well known and had even appeared on Irish TV, but something in my head told me to go and it was easy to get a flight over in the morning and get one back in the afternoon. It wasn't as if it was that far to go.

If I needed any warning that I was playing with fire it came when I got a taxi at the airport. The driver recognised me and started chatting! When he asked where I wanted to go I gave him a location which I knew was quite a way from the shop and then walked the rest of the way. By this time I was determined to go to this place and that seemed to override any thoughts I might have had about being spotted. The staff told me about people who were transitioning and how I could go to Manchester and see a doctor and a counsellor if I was thinking of going down that particular route. Although I was fascinated by the thought of it and what it would mean, I knew there was no way I could even contemplate anything like that.

Yet my thoughts and actions were being driven by my female urges and I wonder if there was actually part of me that wanted to get caught. Perhaps subconsciously I'd become tired with the fight, tired of keeping up the pretence. Maybe part of me thought that if I did get caught at least it would then be out in the open. My female side was slowly but surely gaining the upper hand and in the years which would follow it would become an unstoppable force. Trying to control or contain what was happening would prove futile.

The win in Vegas against Holyfield signalled the beginning of the end for me with Lennox. We'd both set out with our different dreams and we'd managed to realise them. Things change and people move on. I didn't feel it was the same for me and my relationship with Panos seemed to be deteriorating by the day. I can't say it was a particularly pleasant time but I still had a job and I got on with it, even if my enthusiasm wasn't quite the same. A guy called Adrian Ogun began to play an increasing role in Lewis's career. I had first met him some years before when a journalist introduced us, and in 1994 I'd had a breakfast meeting with him about his company, Media Machine, possibly doing some sponsorship work for Lennox. I could tell even back then that he wanted to get involved in the Lewis set-up in some way and that is eventually what happened.

Lennox had three title defences in 2000, of which the first two produced second-round victories – against Michael Grant in New York and Frans Botha in London. By the time the third contest came around against David Tua in Vegas, I had left Panix – the organisation I'd been part of with Panos – and moved to Frank Warren's Sports Network. I was still Lennox's manager for the Tua fight, but it was pretty clear to me that my role had been diminished and I began to feel like an outsider. I instinctively knew my time with Lennox was coming to an end. Lewis beat Tua on points but less than a month after the November fight I was involved in another world title contest, the result of which almost made me walk away from boxing altogether.

I had a whole stable of fighters in addition to Lewis and I put everything I could into making a success of their careers. On the day Lennox fought Holyfield in Vegas, I had spent my afternoon in a Sky television truck listening to the commentary of a fight 6,000 miles away. Paul Ingle, a featherweight from Scarborough I managed, was boxing Manuel Medina for the IBF world title. I had been overjoyed when Paul won the contest with a victory on points. He defended the title against Junior Jones on the same pro-motion which saw Lewis beat Grant in New York and in December 2000 had another defence against a South African fighter called Mbulelo Botile in Sheffield. It turned out to be a horrific night.

Paul was not his usual self in the ring and by the end of the 11th round I knew that the only way he could win was by knock-ing his opponent out but in the next round he was hit by a punch from Botile and collapsed. Paul actually sat up and then rolled over. I knew instantly something terrible had happened. He was in real trouble and had to be rushed to hospital where he had a blood clot removed from his brain. It was a horrible thing to happen and at the time we didn't know whether he would live or die.

Thankfully, he survived the operation and over the years which have followed Paul has needed all the fighting qualities he once showed in the ring to cope with life and a lengthy recovery period. I was stunned by what happened that night and began to question whether boxing was a business I wanted to be involved in any more. The sport can be brutal and everyone is aware there will always be a risk when two fighters step into a ring. I was still badly shaken that Christmas when I went to a party at Eugene's gym, who was now managing and promoting fighters. Some of the boxers I managed were there and told me they knew the risks they took whenever they stepped through the ropes and also that I shouldn't blame myself. It made me feel better and I did carry on, but I'd be lying if I said there weren't some doubts creeping into my thoughts following the events in Sheffield. Paul had realised his dream of becoming a world champion but it had lasted for little more than a year and he paid a terrible price.

Three months later I experienced a very different kind of emotion when I became a father for the third time and once again I had another daughter when little Libby was born in March 2001. She was a beautiful little baby, just as Emma and Sophie had been. Tracey and I were once again proud parents and to the outside world everything must have looked so perfect and settled. Having Libby probably only enhanced my image as the family man and I was happy with my family. I loved Tracey and all three of my children, but there was also a nagging feeling lurking deep inside me about what might lie ahead in both my private and professional lives.

A month after Libby was born, I was in South Africa when Lennox became an ex-champion for the second time in his career. His defeat came at the hands of American Hasim Rahman in the fifth round of their world title fight. A big right-hand punch ended the contest and it was the last Lennox Lewis fight I would be involved in.

Lewis was due to meet Rahman in a re-match in November 2001 but weeks earlier we parted company, after 12 years together as manager and fighter. Of course it was sad in many ways, but looking back, perhaps things had run their course. We had some great times together and I have an awful lot to thank Lennox for but I also like to think I played a real part in helping him reach the top. I never stopped working as hard as I could on his behalf. I can look back now and feel proud of what I did and what I achieved.

The fact that I was able to carry on giving one hundred per cent throughout his career while at the same time trying to deal with my gender issue may seem strange to lots of people. I was part of a very macho world and operated at the highest level in the sport. But I think it was my ability to keep the two sides of my personality apart which enabled me to work and be successful. Having such a busy work schedule was actually a help when it came to dealing with what was going on inside me. Whenever I was working I was totally focussed on the job in hand and I think my record shows I was good at that job. My inner feelings never interfered with my work.

I had been a boxing man long before I became Lennox's manager and when my relationship with him finally ended I decided to carry on. But perhaps that day in 2001 would have been the perfect time to draw a line under things and move away from the sport. I had toyed with the idea of doing just that after the second Holyfield fight, having given some serious thought to my gender problem and what it was doing to me. Whenever my female side took hold of me the thoughts and desires seemed to be stronger than ever. I wondered if it might be better to just take a different path and give in. To allow myself to be the person I thought I always should be and explore the possibility of transitioning.

I had enough money in the bank to not worry about things financially and I knew I would make sure I looked after the family. It would have allowed me to stop living a lie and perhaps lead the life I was always meant to lead. But I didn't do it. I couldn't do it. I wasn't brave enough and the truth is that I also loved a lot of what Frank Maloney was about. I liked being Tracey's husband, I liked being a father to Sophie and Libby and boxing was in my blood.

Yet I began to find it increasingly difficult to carry on as I had done before when it came to my private life. The internet was a constant source of information and the more I discovered the more restless I became within myself. I was becoming difficult to live with and my home life suffered. It got to the point where I began to snap at Tracey for the least little thing and although I knew I was sometimes being unreasonable and difficult, it didn't stop me from behaving in a way that was often selfish. I could be irritable and grumpy. Sometimes I would suffer bouts of depression. I was drinking heavily and often seemed upset with just about everything in my life. I was becoming the sort of person I didn't like, but I did nothing about it – nothing to try and correct my behaviour. Not great for any wife, but if we did have arguments from time to time I would always try to make it up to her in some way.

I would try to make it up to Tracey with gifts or flowers, but what I really should have been doing was talking to her. Part of me wanted to be able to open up and confide in her. To tell her what was going on and why I often felt so moody and acted badly towards her, but as usual I held back. I was like an illusionist who had managed to convince people I was still the happy-go-lucky person they always assumed I was. As miserable and grumpy as I was on occasions, I was still Frank, her husband and the father of her children. The only bit that didn't require any sort of illusion was the inner me to which nobody had access and which was all too real. I now believe that the summer of 2006 was the start of the dismantling of the Frank Maloney everyone knew both publicly and privately. The pressure of what was going on in my head actually led to me having some kind of breakdown.

We'd had a house in Portugal for some years and used to enjoy spending summers there. The kids loved it and it was nice to be able to relax with friends and socialise. I always found going there very relaxing and that year we headed to Portugal as soon as we could. Sophie and Libby loved spending hours in the pool, we would go to the beach to meet a group of people we'd got to know over the years and I loved entertaining at the house and having barbecues.

By this time I had left Sports Network and was running my own business, managing and promoting fighters. I had been involved in a lot of big shows and promotions during my time working with Frank Warren, but just felt I wanted to have my own set-up once more. I was looking forward to the break and we'd also invited two friends from England and their kids to join us for a couple of weeks. It should have been a great chance to unwind and have a proper family holiday away from the stresses and strains of life in England. I wanted to clear my head of some of the mental torment which had clearly started to affect my personality and marriage. Instead, it turned into the holiday from hell for poor Tracey and made me realise I desperately needed to seek help.

One day a row broke out between us after I had been drinking, but that was certainly no excuse for what happened. Tracey and I were in our bedroom and what began as a mild disagreement soon escalated into a full-blown fight between us. I remember losing my temper as I screamed and shouted at her. Within what could only have been a matter of seconds I'd lost control. I don't know exactly what the trigger was. I don't know what was said, all I can remember is a rage building within me until it spilled over and I was out of control. I lunged at Tracey, grabbing her around the neck and in that split-second I was like a man possessed, the outside world didn't exist and the fact that I was acting like a madman meant nothing to me. What brought me back to my senses was the sound of Sophie and Libby's frightened voices.

The girls heard all the noise and wanted to know what was happening. It must have been horrible for them: Libby was just five at the time, but Sophie was 11 and old enough to know that something terrible was happening. My two little girls saw the anger in me and what I was trying to do to their mother. It was awful and if they hadn't come into the room at that point I dread to think what might have happened. My anger seemed to subside just as quickly as I had lost control and I was left with a tremendous feeling of remorse at what I had just done. I couldn't believe my actions. I had been out of control and I could have killed Tracey. I could have killed the woman I loved, in one crazy moment I could have destroyed everything. I tried to say, 'Sorry,' but the atmosphere was too highly charged. I had gone too far and I could see the fear in Tracey's eyes. It was horrible and the haunted look she had as tears rolled down her face was really upsetting. I was shocked by what I had tried to do and what I had become. I was violent and unstable. My mind was all over the place. I knew I had to get out of the house. Get away, for everyone's sake.

I got in my car and just drove. That night I spent about four hours just sitting outside a very old church in a place called Almancil in the Algarve. For four hours I sat there, crying and crying. I prayed and asked God why I was acting in the way I was, what was the matter with me, why I was destroying everything around me? I knew I was in a bad way and although I tried to apologise to Tracey when I got back to the house early the next morning, I knew it was really not going to be good enough. The way I'd behaved had frightened and shocked both of us.

CHAPTER THIRTEEN

Taking the lid off

The holiday in Portugal had brought tensions to the surface with Tracey in the most shocking way possible. The two friends staying with us were a husband and wife we'd known for some years. The husband, Steve, told me I probably needed some professional help after the blazing row I'd had with Tracey. He didn't know what my problem was, but it was obvious to both of us as we sat and chatted that I couldn't carry on ignoring the fact that I'd reached a point where I had to do something about myself. When we travelled back to England; I thought Tracey really wanted out of the marriage, but what had gone on also frightened me. I had been so angry and out of control, and the consequences could have been catastrophic.

I'd managed a fighter who needed help for drug and alcohol problems and he'd gone to a clinic in Sussex for help. I wondered if they'd be able to do something for me with the mental demons I was battling. I'd been behaving badly for months and seemed to feel constantly stressed. I went the clinic knowing I'd been depressed, I was drinking too much for my own good and had an anger issue. I felt as though I was beginning to lose control of my life after fighting so hard and for so many years to stay on top of things. The clinic's treatment included vitamins and minerals, and they suggested it might be a good idea for me to spend time with a counsellor. That was when my problems really began.

The clinic had links with Scientology and the counsellor I saw said she had a lot of experience and mentioned that she'd been used in the aftermath of 9/11 to help people who had been traumatised by their experience of what had happened on that day. She explained that she was going to begin a process which was called auditing. It turned out to be a big mistake. Some of the sessions were incredibly long and at the end I felt totally drained. Maybe some people are helped but that certainly wasn't true in my case.

I stayed at the clinic for about three or four weeks, and Tracey had no idea where I was and neither did my office. I let James Russell, my press officer, know that I was okay and said I wouldn't be around for a while and he acted as a go-between with Tracey. The sessions with the counsellor were really tough and I felt a hypnotic effect as she took me back through my life. I found myself in an almost trance-like state, talking to her about past existences and she explained to me that the spirit never dies but passes into different bodies, living different lives. In each of the lives I told her about I was a female, including being a young Catholic girl who'd had her baby taken away from her. It was a very weird experience and also incredibly emotional. Instead of feeling refreshed and finding an answer to what had been causing my depression and anger, I think I ended up in a worse state than before.

Tracey returned home from a flight one day to find me in the conservatory of our house with the counsellor and some other people from the clinic. She has since told me that when she walked in and saw me I looked as though I was completely out of it, as if I'd been brainwashed. She was just glad that I'd appeared and was in one piece. The woman who had been carrying out the auditing process with me then started to quiz Tracey. She was stunned by being interrogated and having to defend herself in front of this complete stranger. For a time she went along with it, but very quickly realised what a ridiculous situation she found herself in with her own home being taken over. She basically threw them out of the house and told them to get lost, but that wasn't the end of it.

I was in bits. I really couldn't function and I felt incredibly vulnerable. I did carry on seeing the woman from the clinic and even persuaded Tracey that she should go along and see her too but it didn't go well. Tracey said that she hadn't been offered any food or drink during a session that lasted for hours and she also felt that she was under interrogation. In the end it only confirmed what she'd thought from that first meeting in our house, which was that I should wash my hands of the whole process and stop allowing this woman to have so much control in my life. I had lost confidence, as if I'd been stripped of any self-belief.

The counsellor even turned up at my office and was basically trying to tell me how to run things. As for me, I was just going through the motions when it came to my business. I would sit at my desk unable to make any decisions and I think that if it hadn't been for James holding it together, I'd have probably lost everything. I received a bill from her for £5,000 and paid it without querying anything. I was on the floor mentally and not able to think straight.

By now Tracey had told me that it was either the clinic or her. I got another bill from the counsellor and this time it was for £6,500. I don't know if it was the size of the bill that brought me to my senses but a bit of the old Frank returned and I refused to pay. I'd had enough of her and her methods, I felt worse than ever and it was pretty clear the whole process had done me no good at all. I suppose the one thing which had happened was that my anger towards Tracey had gone, simply because I was unable to think straight or function in the way I had in the past. And yet I still felt I needed some sort of help and counselling. We both did if we were going to save our marriage and stay together as a couple. I needed someone who could help me deal with my life and reverse the process I'd been through. I managed to find that person in November 2006.

Her name was Jan who was a life counsellor and from our very first meeting I felt at easy and comforted by what she told me. I explained what had happened and how I had been affected by the process. She explained to me that being the sort of person I was and coming from the kind of business I was in meant I had needed to build a hard exterior in order to operate and function. She tried to explain in very simple terms what she thought had gone on. She used the analogy of a windowsill which had been given several layers of varnish that protected the wood underneath. She told me that what I'd been through with the previous counsellor was the equivalent to that windowsill being stripped of its varnish until the wood was exposed.

'That's the point you're at now,' Jan claimed. 'You've been stripped bare mentally and it's left you feeling very vulnerable.' She was going to try and put a couple of those mental coats of varnish back so that I would be able to start functioning again.

I came out of that first session feeling completely different and confident that I'd managed to find someone who could really be of help to me. Not just me, to Tracey as well because we were going to see her as a couple and also individually. Both of us wanted the marriage to succeed.

But despite the help I was getting from Jan, she – like everyone else in my life – had no idea of my biggest problem. I liked Jan immediately and knew I would be able to open up and unburden myself, but I also realised that would only be up to a point. No matter how much I might have wanted to say something about my secret feminine feelings, I still believed I could never tell anyone without destroying my life. I was probably becoming more concerned with the thoughts I was having. The female in me was not going away, the desire to be a woman was still there. I would get frustrated by the fact that I was finding it harder to deal with the problem and to control it in the way I might have been able to a few years earlier. It made me irritable and depressed. I wasn't great to live with and by the time the end of the year came around, it was clear we had a big decision to make.

That Christmas we decided that we would have a make-or-break holiday in Cancun. So we took the girls off to Mexico and we'd decided that we would try to explain to them what was happening on the last day we were there. We actually thought we would be saying that their mum and dad were splitting up, but it never happened. We never did have that conversation. Instead, we returned to England, both hoping things would improve in the year that was coming up. If I had been honest with myself, I knew that was never likely to be the case. The stress and strain of trying to lead a double life was taking its toll. I was not the person Tracey thought I was and during the holiday there was one incident, that was actually quite funny, which illustrated just how ridiculous my continual cover-up had become.

We were out shopping one day and Tracey picked up a dress in a store and was looking at it. She turned around to see me holding up exactly the same dress, only in a size 14. Not surprisingly, she asked me what I was doing. I made the excuse that it was for a friend of mine who was a nurse back in England and I thought it might make a nice present for her. She thought no more of it, but although I did have a friend who was a nurse, I actually liked the look of it for myself!

The Portugal incident was still fresh in both of our memories and I don't think either of us wanted a repeat performance from me. When I first went to see Jan I explained that I had anger problems, although I wasn't entirely honest about what lay at their root. I still believed that having regular counselling would help Tracey and me cope and stay together and there was no doubt seeing Jan was a big help to both of us, but I also couldn't stop myself from trying to find out more about the gender issue I had by using the internet.

I set up different email accounts and used a variety of names to explore sites and the various chat rooms. I was desperate to know if I really was a transsexual because – crazy as this may sound, given all that had gone on in my life up to this point – I was still hoping that someone somewhere would tell me that I wasn't really transsexual. I was being delusional, but I wanted tests I could do to establish exactly what I was and why I felt the way I did. There was now so much information and I would sit for hours, fascinated by what I was reading, poring over accounts from people who were transsexual. I also came across the names of various gender counsellors to email.

Throughout 2007, there was often a tense atmosphere in the house and I know that at times I must have appeared increasingly distant to Tracey. Somehow or other we both seemed able to present a united front to our family and friends and to the outside world we still looked like a happy couple with two beautiful daughters and a great lifestyle. I even organised a party at our house that year for Tracey's 40th birthday which included hiring a Tom Jones impersonator singing live on the night. She'd always loved the real Tom Jones, so it was just a bit of fun and good entertainment having this guy there. We had lots of friends over and I bet not one of them would have suspected anything was wrong.

By the time the end of the year rolled around, we had decided on another make-or-break holiday and this time it really did look as though it would signal the end for us. It was a case of same idea, different location. Instead of Mexico, we headed off to Vegas, but despite the fact that we both felt we couldn't go on as we were the result was exactly the same as it had been a year earlier and we decided to stay together. I think we were both kidding ourselves, believing we could somehow mend our marriage when it wasn't just broken but smashed to pieces.

I just became more difficult to live with. Nothing seemed to please me and poor Tracey was often treading on eggshells. The least little thing could trigger an argument and I could see that she was beginning to blame herself for the breakdown of our marriage. I could be spiteful and quite vicious and, while it's not a very nice thing to have to admit, I think that in my twisted way of thinking it actually suited me to let her heap blame on herself. I suppose it was another form of protection against the real reason for my unhappiness. The trouble was, I hated seeing what I was doing. I was slowly destroying her. She must have been glad that she still flew part-time and was able to be away on long-haul trips. I still had my boxing business, but it wasn't the same as it had been and I certainly wasn't as rushed off my feet as I had been in the past.

I had too much time on my hands and that wasn't a good thing. I was still going to my counselling sessions and I found them useful, but I came out of them knowing that I hadn't told Jan the real reason for my unhappiness. The effect was to make me more depressed and anxious. I'd kept a lid on things for my entire life. I was 55 years old and no matter how much I wanted to kid myself into believing otherwise, my gender dysphoria wasn't going to go away or be cured. I had been born into the wrong body, I was a woman struggling to come to terms with what nature had dealt me. It was causing me mental torture and I wasn't sure where it would all end, but it had nothing to do with Tracey. She had just been unlucky to be caught up in something she knew nothing about. She was on the receiving end and she didn't deserve that. I had tried to be strong throughout our time together and battled against my inner feelings, but that strength was really a weakness because it meant I never owned up to myself. I was being a coward and it had gone on for long enough.

I was never the sort of person who has a solid eight hours sleep a night. Partly because of my work and partly because of the way I was built, I'd often sleep for a few hours and then be wide awake at the best of times. But during this period my sleep pattern was all over the place. I'd find myself pacing around, as my mind went into overdrive. I knew I couldn't go on hiding things from Tracey any longer. I thought I could carry on dealing with my problem but the truth was I couldn't and it had been stupid to think I could. The last couple of years had been a nightmare for Tracey because of the way I'd acted towards her. I knew that taking hormones might be a way of helping me in my day-to-day existence and with the chemical balance within my body. I started to take some of Tracey's birth control pills, without her knowing.

One night it came to a head after we'd had yet another row and I'd even told her she wasn't a good wife, which was so unfair. The truth was that I wasn't a good husband or, at least, not an honest one. We had been sleeping in separate rooms for some time but I knew I was probably keeping Tracey awake with the way I was pacing around. She was due to fly the next morning to Vegas and I knew she would need to get a good night's sleep because she was going to be working for 11 hours, but my mind was in turmoil. I couldn't stand it any longer and went to her room. She could see I was already upset as I sat at the end of her bed.

'I've got something I need to tell you,' I said, as tears began to run down my cheeks. I knew that within seconds both of our lives would change forever. I was going to deliver a verbal bomb that would blow our marriage to pieces. Things would never be the same between us and I was about to destroy the woman I had loved for 15 years.

I would be lying if I said I could remember the exact words I used to explain to her that I was, and always had been, a woman trapped in a man's body. That I had lived a lie all of my life and that I wanted to be a female. What I do remember is wishing I could take the words back as they came tumbling out of my mouth. I could see from the shock and hurt in her eyes that what I'd said had devastated her. She looked upset and bewildered as she tried to come to terms with what I'd said. She knew I had been acting strangely. Knew I had been depressed and angry. Knew there was a problem, but could never have imagined exactly what that problem was, and that the reason our marriage wasn't working was because of me and not her.

I felt a mixture of horror and relief at what I had just done, but there was no going back. The secret I had kept from her was out in the open now. We sat on the end of the bed clinging to each other for emotional and physical support as we sobbed in each other's arms. The last few minutes had drained us. I had turned Tracey's world upside down and now we both had to try and come to terms with the consequences of what had happened. We went downstairs to the kitchen, made tea and talked for ages, but I knew we could have talked for days and still not been able to say all the things we wanted to. We were both exhausted, but it was good to finally have an honest conversation with Tracey.

I don't know how she did it, but at 6.00 am Tracey went off to spend 11 hours in the air on a flight to the USA. She could see how upset I was as she left the house but made me promise to hold things together in front of the girls while she was away. She said we would talk more when she got back. Tracey has since told me that, understandably, she was in bits too that morning and that several times during the long flight to the USA she had to lock herself in the toilet as she cried her way across the Atlantic.

Although telling Tracey was a relief in many ways, it also meant that I had created another problem. For as long as I could remember I had kept my gender dysphoria a secret. Now I had burdened Tracey with the same secret and I realised just how difficult life was going to be for her and for us. Telling Tracey didn't give us a fresh start but instead began the long and, at times, painful disintegration of our marriage. She couldn't tell the kids or any of her own family. She couldn't talk about it to any of our friends. I had given myself some mental relief in telling her but now she had to keep my secret while trying to maintain a normal exterior.

I needed some time on my own. My life seemed like such a mess and I was feeling quite depressed. The house in Portugal had always held happy memories for me and, after Tracey got back from Vegas, I decided to go there to give myself time to think. I felt my spirits lift as soon as I walked through the front door but that feeling soon changed. I sat in a chair and began to think. I wondered what the hell I had done and how I was now going to cope. I was certain that having told Tracey, our relationship would now be over. I also knew that my inner feelings of wanting to be a woman were getting stronger. It wasn't going to get any easier – instead, things were only going to get worse. I sat in the chair as darkness fell. I couldn't be bothered switching a light on. As it got darker outside the house my mood darkened as I sat motionless inside. I began to cry; everything seemed so hopeless. I couldn't see how I was going to carry on. I started to think about taking my own life as at least then I would be able to escape from my problems. I wanted to be a woman but couldn't be one. I wanted to dress as a woman and feel comfortable. I wanted to be myself. Eventually the tears stopped and I pulled myself together. I'd had black moods before and come out of them and this time I comforted myself with the thought of a shopping trip in the nearby city of Faro the next day.

I had sometimes bought women's clothes and make-up in the past but I had never kept any. I would think about how I would like to look with my new purchases but then I would stuff all the shopping back into bags and chuck them away. But when I decided to go to Faro I had no intention of throwing away any of the clothes I was going to buy. I also hunted around for a wig and some make-up and as soon as I got back to the house I began to try the clothes on. I sat in front of a mirror, put on make-up and the wig. I looked at my reflection. I was fully dressed as a woman and I felt happy. I'd bought a variety of clothes, some for dressing up, some for sitting around, but all were for women. Being able to sit and relax, watching television fully dressed as a female, felt really good.

Tracey called one day and we chatted for quite a while. She asked me if I was really serious about what I'd said. I'm sure she was still in shock in many ways, but I told her that I was serious and explained that it wasn't something which had just happened. I'd been living with it for my entire life. As I talked to her I looked down at myself. Tracey had no way of knowing, but I was sitting there talking to her fully dressed as a woman. I knew there was no going back and, the tears began to fall down my face once more. My emotions were all over the place.

A few months before telling Tracey about myself I had made contact via the internet with a gender specialist, a Dr Leslie. He was English but based in south-east Asia and all his consultations were done online. I used an assumed name and paid in euros through a separate account I had set up. I found the whole thing very useful and he was able to answer a lot of my questions and explained things in a very straightforward way. At this time I was feeling very depressed and uncomfortable with what was going on with Tracey and me. Dr Leslie understood how I felt and I knew I wasn't the first person to ask him about my dilemma. I suppose I wanted reassurance about taking that massive step in telling her. I wanted to know how she might react, but I suppose I knew there was no set pattern or rules when it came to telling your partner. I remember him telling me that once I had made that decision, there was no going back. Tracey and I continued to present a united front to the world, but far from helping us when we were at home, things only seemed to get worse, and there was only one reason for that. Me.

I can only shudder at what I put Tracey through. There she was being the happy wife for family and friends, a mother to Sophie and Libby, she had her flying career, and she had to carry on with all of this knowing her husband wanted to be a woman. Instead of showing sympathy and compassion, I became more distant and retreated into myself. I may have shared my biggest secret with her but that didn't mean I was going to open up and I didn't think she would like to hear more of my thoughts and feelings. On occasions we would be just as spiteful to each other as we had been before she knew about me.

When it came to an argument neither of us backed down easily and there were some horrible moments when we would just hurl hurtful words at each other which we both regretted the instant we'd said them. It was an indication of the underlying tension that existed between us. I tried to bury myself in work but at the same time I was leading a very different second life to anything I had experienced before, as the urge to explore the transgender world began to increase. I couldn't stop myself. This thing was too powerful and too strong. If I thought I could still manage and contain the way I felt, I was clearly kidding myself. But in a way, that's just what I did. I would go to work, managing boxers, organising shows and trying to make the business work during what were very difficult times.

If you are going to succeed in boxing you always need to have fighters who are potential champions and the sort of stars who will go all the way to the top and be the main attraction on any promotion. Lennox Lewis had won the Olympics in Seoul as an amateur and in 2008 an Irish fighter named Darren Sutherland competed in the Beijing Olympics. He was a middleweight and he returned to his native Ireland as a bronze medallist. Darren was very good and appeared to have everything he needed to reach the very top.

I was lucky enough to sign him to a professional contract, although in the end I invested nearly £100,000 of my own money to make sure he became one of my fighters. Darren was a lovely guy and my family really liked him as well. In fact, he spent quite a few months living with us and he was good to have around. When he signed, he got money, a car and a flat. I wanted to make sure he felt as comfortable and happy as possible.

He had his first professional fight in December 2008, winning in the opening round and then had three more victories in 2009, the last of which was against Ukrainian Gennadiy Rasalev at the end of June. Darren won in the fourth round and it was to be his last ever contest. On Monday 14 September I went to his flat in Bromley and found him dead. He had committed suicide by hanging himself.

It was an absolute tragedy and a day I will never forget. Less than 48 hours earlier he had been out for a Chinese meal with me, Tracey and the two girls. He'd been chatting to Sophie and Libby about TV programmes and seemed to be enjoying himself. We'd asked him if he wanted to stay at our place, he hadn't wanted to and that was the last time I was to see him alive.

A few days earlier, he had come to my office and basically told me that he didn't want to box any more. Joe Dunbar – a sports physiologist who had worked with many of my fighters over the years, including Lennox Lewis – had been working with Darren and had told me this might be the case. We arranged to meet in my office to sort things out. Although I'd had high hopes for Darren, there was no way I was ever going to force him to box against his will. I said we would have to come to some sort of agreement about the money he'd been given, but that kind of thing could be worked out. The important thing was that Darren did what he felt comfortable with.

On the day before we went for the meal, Joe spoke to Darren on the phone and got the impression that all was not well. Joe thought it best to get an appointment with a clinical psychologist and that was fixed for the following Monday. I didn't hear from Darren on Sunday and Joe tried calling him that day without any success. Joe became increasingly concerned and on the Monday morning he phoned to say he was going to Darren's flat to see if there was anything wrong. We met at the flat but neither of us had a key and we had to call the landlord to arrange for one. We waited for quite a long time before the landlord arrived and we were able to get in. Joe went into one room and I went into another.

The sight that greeted me was just horrible. Darren was there, lifeless, without any expression on his face. The same Darren who had been happily talking to Sophie and Libby less than two days earlier. I just couldn't comprehend what had happened and began to shout for Joe. I went into shock. It was just totally overwhelming. For a while I couldn't think straight and everything was a blur. Even now I can't quite remember what happened. I was just grateful that Joe was with me, because he kind of took control of the situation and phoned the police.

Darren was just 27 years old and had his life in front of him, but he clearly had his own demons to deal with and tragically they got the better of him. In his flat, I apparently lost all colour from my face and began sweating. I ended up being checked over because one of the ambulance crew who were there could see there was clearly something wrong with me. They decided to take me to the Princess Royal hospital in Bromley.

I was hooked up to all sorts of monitoring equipment and I was still in a daze. Finding Darren had been a massive shock, but it wasn't long before the staff at the hospital delivered another. I was told that I'd suffered a heart attack, I was kept in and put under observation over night. The tests they carried out revealed the heart attack had actually occurred a few days earlier when I'd been watching one of my fighters, John McDermott, lose to Tyson

Fury in Brentwood. At the time I hadn't been able to believe the decision and I thought it was an absolute travesty. I went mad, claiming McDermott should have won it and I could feel a tightness in my chest and a bit of pain, but I put it down to the fact that I was angry and stressed at what had gone on in the ring.

That was the trigger, but I was also carrying around a lot of mental baggage – almost a year on from the time I had come clean with Tracey, things had really got no better between us. We were trying to stay together and make the marriage work in some way and we were friends. I was grateful for what she was doing for me in keeping my secret safe, but it was hard for both of us to carry on as though everything was fine.

I had an uneventful night at the hospital, but the next day brought fresh drama when my heart actually stopped beating for about 30 seconds. It was a very strange experience for me. I could feel the medical people pushing down on my chest and then – nothing. I didn't hear anything, but I remember feeling incredibly comfortable and contented. I know it's been said before by other people under similar circumstances, but I really do believe I had some form of out-of-body experience.

I had to be rushed to King's College hospital for them to operate on me before being transferred back to the Princess Royal. Within 24 hours I was sitting up in my bed and driving everyone mad as I tried to work from my laptop and use my mobile. To everyone I was in typical Frank Maloney mode, but what had happened in the space of a few days did have a sobering effect on me. It couldn't fail to and, with time on my hands as I sat in hospital, I began to wonder if the death of Darren and my heart attack might be some sort of sign. Perhaps I should stop fighting things every step of the way and instead finally start to change my life forever.

CHAPTER FOURTEEN

Unhappy Christmas

My life started to change after my heart attack but it was a slower process than I'd thought it would be. I was still trying to perform my old trick of juggling two lives. No matter how much I might have liked the thought of just giving in and simplifying things by going down the route I knew I should, the Frank in me was still playing a significant role: as they were wheeling me down to the operating theatre after I'd been diagnosed, I still found time to make sure I'd signed a promising heavyweight from Liverpool named David Price.

Perhaps, having had the heart attack, it would have been a good moment to call it a day and slowly disappear from the sport, just as I thought I might do after Lewis beat Holyfield and again when Lennox and I went our separate ways. I certainly knew that, initially, I had to take things easy after the scare I'd had, but it wasn't long before I was back in the office and trying to work as I always had done. It also wasn't long before I had slipped back into the uneasy atmosphere of life at home with Tracey and the girls.

She had been really good to me with my health problems and I knew I had her love and support, but I still made things difficult for her by the way I behaved. I still had periods of depression and I also had moments of anger. Tracey might have known why I acted in the way I did, but the girls didn't and all they would hear on occasions was their mum and dad having another shouting match.

Sometimes it was easier for both of us when I was at work. Signing David certainly had an invigorating effect because I had always liked looking after heavyweights. I'd had my biggest success with Lewis, but there had been others along the way. They might not have become as successful but I like to think I helped them to fulfil their potential in terms of what they achieved and the money they earned as professionals. So perhaps taking on David Price was a sign that I shouldn't walk away from boxing but try to guide his career in the best way I could. I honestly thought that, given the luck you always need in sport, I could help get David Price to the very top and I still found the thought of that exciting. I was proud of my achievements and status within boxing. So too was my dad.

Just like my mother, he had followed my career from the very early days and both of them were delighted to see me make such a success of my career. I knew it meant a lot to my dad and I got a very warm feeling from seeing his eyes light up whenever I visited him in his favourite pub. He would immediately make a fuss of me and introduce me to all of his friends and as many people as he could in the bar. I remembered all those chats he would have about working hard and getting on in life. How he had his clearly defined rules about what a man should be and the way he should act. To him I'd probably fulfilled all of those hopes and ideals. I'd worked hard, earned money, been a success, bought houses, had nice cars, been married, had three beautiful daughters and provided for my family. In his eyes I was everything a man should be, except that for my entire life I had known different and if my father had known that same truth I was convinced our relationship would have ended. It would have been too much for him to take and it would have gone against everything he thought his eldest son should be. My dad had his faults just like anyone else and although he had never found it easy to talk about emotional things or just give me a hug, I always knew he loved me and that we had a bond. He was a macho type of man and thought I was exactly the same.

By 2010 my dad's health was beginning to fade. It became apparent that time was running out for him and in May he died. Losing your father is a terrible moment for any son and it was no different for Eugene, Vince and me. My dad had been a larger-than-life character in all of our lives and suddenly he was gone. It was upsetting and sad, and I think it left a void in all our lives. His death had a particular effect on me, somehow making my inner feelings more intense. While he was alive I was always trying to be the son he wanted, trying to live up to what he expected. I can't say for certain what his reaction would have been if I'd told him, but I can guess. I don't think it would really have been his fault, I just think it was the way he was built. My dad was a good man and a good father, I loved him and I know he loved me. I think I made him proud and happy while he was alive and I'm grateful his image of me wasn't shattered. Whatever was going on inside me at the time, I know he saw me as his son until the day he died.

It hadn't been easy for me or any of the family to see my dad's health begin to deteriorate and that was certainly true for Emma.

Like any granddaughter, Emma loved her grandfather, or Gramps as she called him, as did all of his grandchildren. She had always visited him regularly and she was there for him when he became ill. My own relationship with Emma hadn't always been so easy.

We had a special bond when Emma was a little girl. I used to love to have her with me and when Jackie and I split up I was glad she ended up living with me. She had always been so protective of me even when she was just a kid and when she lived with me I remember her actually kicking out a girlfriend I'd brought home one evening! She was strong-willed and independent and by the time she was 17 she was renting her first house and had a good job. She got on with her life and although it was a bit of a shock for me to get the news at the time, she had her first child, Robyn, shortly after Tracey gave birth to Sophie, I became a father and a grandfather in the space of about nine months.

Over the next few years Emma married and had a son, Ollie, and although I never fell out with her, our relationship became a bit strained and volatile. We were both stubborn people and maybe she had quite a few of the characteristics I could see in myself. She certainly wasn't the sort of person to back down and neither was I. One day a disagreement on the phone ended with us not being in contact again for six years. It was crazy and a terrible thing for me to do. I can see that so clearly now. I couldn't see it then and it just goes to show how stupid I was. For six years I lost my daughter, I lost my Emms. One day I phoned to thank her for being so supportive of my dad. It was the first time we had spoken for six years. As the tears flowed on both ends of the phone I knew I desperately wanted my eldest daughter back in my life and I cursed the fact that we had ever fallen out in the first place.

We arranged to meet for a coffee and slowly began to repair our relationship. It was so important to me and I know the same applied to her. During the time we were not speaking Emma had got divorced and things had changed in her life, I didn't really know my grandchildren and they didn't know their grandfather. I think our not talking also upset my dad and he was forever trying to get the two of us to see reason and speak to each other. The good thing was that we repaired the relationship before he died and it was certainly nice for me to finally have Emma back in my life.

The sad thing was that although I had Emma back, I could not be totally honest with her. She knew nothing about my transgender issues. To her I was the same old dad she'd known all her life with all the faults I'd always had, except that the more she saw of me, the more she could see how angry and frustrated I seemed to be with things at certain times. Like everyone else she probably put it down to my work and my life in general. I spent a lot of time beating myself up mentally but once my father died my desire to live as a woman increased without me being conscious of it.

My continued reluctance to own up fully to what I was and to the route I really should take led to all sorts of mood swings, anger and frustration. If I read something from Dr Leslie that I didn't like I'd basically tell him he didn't know what he was talking about, which was silly, but it was my way of hitting out and denying what was really happening. I searched the internet for other gender counsellors and came across a group of doctors in Argentina. They also could help people when it came to wanting to fully transition. I filled in all sorts of questionnaires and they told me that a mild form of hormone treatment might help me. I think I really wanted them to tell me that I wasn't a transsexual, that with some help I could control this whole thing and manage it. I was looking for anything that might help. The truth was that by 2010 whatever was within me wasn't going to go away.

By the time my father died Tracey had known about my gender issue for more than 18 months. We had both been seeing Jan for a long time and now we weren't doing it as a couple, she was seeing us as individuals. Tracey wanted me to tell Jan. She felt that for us to both move forward, we needed to have someone we could trust and who would be able to take on board exactly what was going on with me. Jan knew we had marriage problems and I'd told her right from the start that I had anger problems, but she knew nothing about what was really the cause of so much of that anger. It wasn't right that I kept going to see her, opening up on all sorts of matters that concerned me and yet kept back the biggest problem of all, so one day I told her.

I just went to see her as I normally would do and then said that I had something to tell her. I blurted out the fact that I was really a transsexual. I had been born into the wrong body and I knew that I was really a woman. As I told her I began to cry. I felt relief at letting her know, but I also felt guilt at not letting her know sooner. I should have told her. I trusted her, she had really helped me and yet I wasn't brave enough to help her. How could I expect her to get to the root of my problem if I wasn't completely honest with her? She told me that she knew I had been holding something back but that it wasn't her job to keep asking. She needed me to open up and tell her when I wanted to do that, and I had obviously reached that point. I knew that from now on I would be able to talk freely about all sorts of issues without having to worry about keeping up the Frank Maloney image.

I think telling Jan was another stage in becoming the person I wanted to be and should be. I continued to communicate with others on the internet. I learned so much from online chats with transsexual girls who could explain things in a very practical way and then make suggestions about other sites and people who might be of help. Then there was Dr Leslie, who suggested making contact with various people he had as clients. One of them, Holly, proved to be really helpful and became a friend. We ended up talking for ages when we first chatted and I described myself to her as a 'closet transgender'. She was really understanding.

Holly suggested I relieve the stress and pressure I was feeling by going to a dressing service. Somewhere I could go and relax, socialising with other people who were like me. She told me about one place in the East End of London but I decided the chances of someone recognising me around there were too high. She mentioned another one which was on the south coast, I checked out the site and got the number to phone. I spoke to a woman called Linda who immediately sounded kind and very understanding. I told her that I was transgender but for years had kept it closeted away, continually fighting it, but I now felt that I needed to express it more and come to terms with who I really was.

Linda said that I could go to see her and that for a very reasonable fee I could dress and have a makeover. All I would do was sit around chatting and having a coffee. It all sounded very informal and relaxed, and also seemed very reassuring. Just the sort of thing I needed to hear. The next stage was summoning up enough courage to make the trip down there and put aside my fears of being recognised.

I booked to go during June 2011, when I was still living at home with Tracey and the girls. The atmosphere at home really hadn't improved – if anything, it had got worse and nobody was benefitting from it. Although I'd told Tracey, I still wasn't being completely honest with her because she didn't know anything about me wanting to dress. I'd occasionally disappeared to Portugal and dressed in female mode while I was out there and I felt incredibly relaxed and happy. It felt so normal for me to dress as a woman but the results were not always what I wanted. I didn't really have the know-how or experience of being able to put my make-up on and I was also experimenting with different dresses. Sometimes I looked in the mirror and thought I looked ugly or that I looked more like a man in a dress than a woman. It wasn't the way I wanted to look, but in many ways I was playing catch-up. I had no real experience of being a woman, and it wasn't just about the way I looked, it was also about things like walking, sitting, talking and mannerisms. I'd read books on make-up, but apart from the times when I'd used dressing services, I had spent my life being a man. If now, as I truly believed, I really was a woman trapped in a man's body then to break free of that body I would need some help and perhaps visiting Linda could be the first stage in that process.

When the day arrived for me to travel to my appointment I was nervous but also excited. I was also paranoid about being recognised. I wore dark glasses and a big scarf which I wrapped around my neck and the lower part of my face. I parked some way from where her house was and then walked to her front door. When she opened it and said, 'Hello,' I immediately felt more comfortable.

I introduced myself as Kellie and Linda was really nice and quickly made me feel more relaxed. I think she could tell I was nervous and wanted to reassure me about what I was doing. Linda wasn't transgender but a genetic woman who just happened to run this particular service. She had a nice house in a nice road and it felt just like popping over to see a friend. I could tell she didn't recognise me which meant I'd got over the first hurdle and when she asked what I did for a living, I said I was in sports management, specialising in staging various events.

I'd brought some clothes with me that I'd had in Portugal and she helped me dress and put on my make-up. She also had a large selection of hairpieces and helped me choose one. When I looked at myself in the mirror I could see her attention had made me very different. I was much more the way I felt I should be and I relaxed even more. We sat in her lounge drinking tea and chatting. She told me a bit about herself and how her ex-partner was transgender. It was good to be able to talk to her about the way I felt and she told me that, in her experience, once the sort of inner feelings I had took a grip on a person they weren't going to go away. It was something I had to come to terms with and deal with.

Linda knew all about the transsexual and transvestite worlds, and told me that she ran regular social evenings at her house where I could get dressed and chat to other people over a drink and some food. She said that maybe I'd like to come to one of them and see what I thought, but I explained that I was scared of being recognised. Linda said I could arrive early, she would get me ready and then I could wait until everyone had gone before I got changed and left for the night. I told her I'd think about it and, after cancelling on the first occasion, I did go along to one of her evenings. It proved to be a real education and eye-opener.

I got to her house early and Linda did a good job of getting me ready and helping me to relax. In the end there were about a dozen people there and I was certainly the most nervous. In complete contrast to the brash Frank Maloney who would take charge of a press conference or give countless television interviews, I just sat there in the corner of the room like a wallflower. I wanted to take everything in, because in many ways it was a surprise.

I looked at all the other people and listened to them talking, but didn't say too much myself. I was still conscious that someone might recognise my voice or that it just wouldn't sound right. I heard these people talking about their family lives and their various businesses. It seemed that most of them were transvestites, although there were a couple who would have liked to have gone all the way and transitioned but for different reasons they couldn't. It felt very strange sitting there quietly and hearing these snatches of conversation, and I suddenly thought to myself, what kind of world am I trapped in?

I came to the conclusion that I didn't really know what to do, didn't know what I wanted to be and, listening to some of the other people, I felt I could end up with losing everything. Yet I did feel comfortable in the way I was dressed and looked. Over three or four hours I started to chat to a few people. It was strange – some of the guests had been dressing far longer than me and been going to these events for some time, but I felt I was further down the line. I already knew the path I wanted to take and yet I still had trouble convincing myself that I should take it.

Linda had been really good and I got on well with her and knew she could be trusted. After all, her whole business depended on trust. I also knew that she definitely had no idea at all who I was. One day we met for a coffee when she told me that she was planning to have a dinner party and there were only going to be eight people invited. She wanted me to be one of them. It was lovely of her to invite me, but I told her I wouldn't be going. I knew in my mind that whatever was inside of me was unstoppable and yet I still wanted to stop it. Something was telling me I was still Frank Maloney, not a woman called Kellie. I still had my business, I had a television contract with Sky, and I had the really crazy notion that perhaps there was a chance of saving my marriage.

'Look Linda, I'm not going to dress anymore,' I told her.

'If that's what you want,' Linda said sympathetically and smiled.

'I don't know if that's what I want,' I admitted, 'but I know that's what I've got to do. I've got to beat it. I don't want to lose my family, my children. I've got quite a successful business and I know that if I continue to transition I'm going to lose everything.'

I thanked Linda for all she'd done for me and the way she had been so kind and helpful. I wished her all the best. Two days later I was on the phone, asking if it would still be possible for me to go to the dinner party. That was how screwed up I was over the whole thing.

I went to the party and enjoyed the evening. I was the last person to leave and as I was taking off my make-up, Linda asked how I felt. I told her I wasn't sure. 'Kellie, I've told you before, if it's that strong in you, you'll never beat it,' she reminded me. After visiting Linda I was more confident in my female mode than I had ever been before. She encouraged me without ever being pushy. She was just there to lend support if I needed it and to advise me with things like my general dress and make-up. That world was now becoming more familiar and I felt I was learning more about myself and just what it meant to be a transsexual.

She did discover who I really was some time later when she saw me in a documentary about promoter Barry Hearn but I knew there was no way she would ever let anyone else know and, far from being panicked, I actually felt comfortable with her knowing my true identity. Over a period of time Linda was to become a great help on my voyage of discovery. She arranged for us to go to various social events, such as the Enigma Ball – which was very well-known within the transgender community.

We travelled to the ball at Bletchley Park, Milton Keynes. Once again I was terrified of being caught out. I couldn't afford to drive up there dressed because I was frightened of being seen if I had a problem with the car. I went in my male clothes with the dark glasses and scarf firmly in place. Just about the only bit of my face you could clearly see was my nose. We'd booked the room at the hotel under Linda's name and the plan was to go out to a club on the night we arrived called Pink Punters. I clearly had been worried because I'd packed clothes for the weekend but forgotten to pack my hairpiece. My first thought was that the weekend was going to be a disaster, but Linda knew someone who was able to provide one and we slowly got ready for the night ahead. I'd experienced all sorts of pressurised situations in my professional life in which I'd managed to conquer my nerves but as we walked into the club I wasn't sure that was going to be the case on this particular occasion. I was shaking. I found myself a corner which seemed out of the way and sat quietly, trying to take everything in.

For a long time all I did was people watch. I looked at all the girls and how they were dressed, and I also looked at the men who were attracted to the girls. These men were known as 'admirers' and once again I found myself in a whole new world. We only stayed for about an hour and I think Linda could see I felt a bit uncomfortable. It was a relief to get back to the hotel room and get some sleep, but the next morning brought a new wave of panic when she said that we were going to go out shopping.

I wasn't sure I was ready to do something like that but she convinced me that because of my size there was no way people were going to stare. She said I was lucky because I could just blend in. One of the biggest fears of any transsexual is that of being 'read', being seen as a man dressed as a woman or, put simply, a bloke in a dress. Happily, I passed the test and with it came more confidence to act and dress the way I always felt I should have.

After shopping came a lunch date with other girls who were quite flamboyant and happy to have their pictures taken. I stayed well clear of any photographs. But it was a good day and I felt quite relaxed out and about, just like any other woman going shopping on a Saturday afternoon. As soon as we got back to the hotel the realisation hit me that we were going to the ball that night and the nerves returned. Perhaps it was having a relaxing day shopping with Linda or maybe it was just that I had quite a few glasses of wine, but as it turned out, I was calmer at the ball than I had been the night before.

Once again I tried to take everything in and I couldn't believe how good looking and elegant some of the girls looked and there were also others who seemed quite outrageous in the way they dressed. Some just looked like men, despite the fact that they were dressed as women. There was a real mix of people, including couples – either a transvestite or a transsexual with their admirer, who could be either male or female. I have to say that I found the male admirers quite strange. This was my first experience of them and there was a question they seemed to want an early answer to. 'Are you pre-op or post-op?' I would say that I was pre-op and then they would ask if I was going to go all the way – was I going to fully transition? When I said that I did intend to, they would say, 'Yes, but you won't be a special woman.' Put very basically these guys wanted you to look like a woman, but still have a penis. I was amazed. There might be a new world opening up for me but there were parts that I found strange and I really didn't want get involved in.

Some of the other girls have since become friends. I wasn't looking for anything sexual – as far as I was concerned, it was all about my gender and trying to correct what had been wrong at birth. Linda knew this and also realised that I was taken aback by things I was hearing about. She told me that as well as the sort of service she offered, there were other places where it was all about sex. It made me realise how broad the transgender world was. I didn't have a problem with that but I knew that it wasn't for me.

I took myself off to New York late in 2011 to Miss Vera's Finishing School for Boys who Want to be Girls. It was a place that provided instruction on dressing and how to look and behave as a woman, including things like walking in high heels. I thought it would be a big help and it was nice to be away from England for a short break in a city I had always loved. It was at Miss Vera's that I first had my picture taken as Kellie and I walked around the streets and went for a meal in my female mode. It gave me a lot of confidence.

As an example of just how strange my life had become at this point, my visit came just about a month after I had walked up the aisle with Emma when she married her second husband, Rich. It was a wonderful occasion and I was such a proud dad. I liked Rich and Emma looked so beautiful and was so happy. We had some lovely pictures taken and there are some special ones with just Emma and me in them, a daughter with her dad. To everyone I was my usual Frank Maloney self and I was genuinely happy. Emma's wedding made me forget my cares and how I was trying to hold everything together. She did not know it, but her father was fast moving towards the day he would become a woman. By now it was just a question of time.

The next step for me was moving out of the house. Trying to live two lives was killing me, but Tracey, the girls and I had gone on holiday to Portugal that year and I thought it would give me more time to think. The holiday turned out to be a disaster and it only became more evident that there was no real future for Tracey and me if we stayed together. She told me that I had to sort myself out otherwise we would destroy each other. She was right but it wasn't pleasant to hear the truth. The conversation got very emotional and I knew I needed to give us both some space.

I moved to Worthing with my two airedale dogs, Winnie and Louie. I'd always loved the idea of living by the coast, I could get back to my office in Kent pretty easily and it wasn't too far from Linda. The first flat I looked at was rented out by a couple of gay guys. They wanted more than I was prepared to pay each month, so I suggested we toss a coin and I ended up winning. They were nice guys and we had a pleasant time chatting. A few hours later the estate agent phoned and told me that one of the guys thought he recognised me and they'd done an internet search before coming up with all the Wikipedia information on me. Part of that information had a section about me making homophobic remarks. They had come from when I'd run for the Mayor of London and made some remarks, actually in jest, which I should never have said. It was wrong and I certainly regret it now, but it was exactly the sort of remark Frank Maloney would have made. Did I do it to just for effect and to add more bricks to the wall I had constructed to protect the person I really was? I don't know, but I suspect there might have been an element of that.

I asked for the number of the guy who had Googled me and I told him that, yes, I was Frank Maloney and, yes, I had made those remarks but I certainly wasn't homophobic. I asked him if he thought I came across as such. He agreed that they both thought I was a nice guy and that we'd all got on well. I told him I loved their flat and was looking forward to moving in. Unfortunately, a week or so later their proposed move fell through and they had to stay in the flat.

I soon managed to find another place not too far away. The down side was that the landlord and a couple of neighbours recognised me. I was still quite self-conscious about being recognised. By this time I had a small collection of female clothes that I kept with Linda but once I got my own flat I moved them,

165

so I was obviously concerned about making sure my life on the coast would be as private as possible. It worked well for six months and then I got the chance to move into another flat in a better location, only to later have problems because there was a mix-up over not being able to have dogs.

I would still see Tracey and the girls. My office wasn't far from the house and it often worked out well because I was able to stay there when Tracey was away on one of her flying trips. It was strange, because the house had always been a special place for me. It was the family home that I'd always wanted. It had a lot of very good memories, but it had also taken on a very different feel in more recent years. Since that day in 2008 when I sat on Tracey's bed and told her just what my problem was, it had never been quite the same. It had been a slow and often painful process for both of us and in many ways I'd ruined Tracey's life. It wasn't nice to have to admit that was the case but it was true. She'd put her life on hold for me and I knew that she would never tell a soul about my secret. She'd carry it to the grave rather than say anything but it wasn't easy for her to protect me in the way she did, particularly with the kids.

When the girls saw me I was often depressed and stressed. Business wasn't great for me and I'd lost the contract with Sky, which was a real blow. I wasn't really functioning in the office. I would often spend a lot of time on my own with the door shut looking at transgender websites and reading magazines on the subject. I hadn't taken my eye off the ball when it came to my business but I certainly wasn't as focussed or driven as I'd been in the past.

By this time Emma had come to work with me, helping with the business and it was good to have her there, although I know that on occasions she must have wondered what the hell was going on with me. I could be very difficult to be around and had some very black moments. I had mood swings and little things would blossom in my head and become big things. I'd sit in my office all alone and my mind would race. I'd start to think of all the possibilities and scenarios there might be for me and what was to come. How what I was doing would ultimately affect all the people who were closest to me and how I could live with what I was doing. I did feel guilty, not for being transgender, but for what it might do to others. In the summer of 2012 I took my first steps to becoming a woman when I went to see a doctor at a private transgender clinic in London. By November I had begun to take hormones. As far as I was concerned there was now no turning back.

I felt I needed to get away to Portugal for a while. As usual, arriving at the house had the calming effect it always seemed to. While I was there I sent some texts to Tracey and we spoke. I told her that I really didn't think I could stop what I was going to do. The urge to become a woman was too strong and powerful. I wasn't going to be able to prevent it. I also told her how sorry I was that this had all happened and made her life so difficult.

'I want you to have a life,' I told her and felt very emotional knowing that I was saying this to the woman I loved and still cared for.

Not long after that conversation I received a text from her that left me devastated and angry. I'd said I wanted her to be honest with me about what was happening with her. If she was going to meet someone else I wanted to know about it. Tracey's text reminded me that I'd asked her to be honest and went on to say she had recently met someone. I realise that I had no right to be angry. I was the person who had shattered her world and made life hell for her. She had every right to try and move on from the wreckage I'd caused but when I got the text my emotions were all over the place and I replied with some bitter messages. I wanted to know how long she had been seeing this new guy and whether I knew him.

By this time I think Tracey was probably regretting ever having told me. I'd said I thought she needed to move on and yet when she took her first steps in doing that, I exploded. Perhaps part of me was jealous, but I think it was more a case of me being faced with the reality of the situation. As daft as it might sound and despite all that had happened since I'd first told Tracey more than four years earlier, I still wanted her in my life, but I'd put her in a prison without bars and forced her to live a lie as well. In many ways it was cruel.

A few weeks before Christmas I arrived at the office in a bit of a state and Emma could see there was something wrong with me. I told her that Tracey and I were splitting up. She knew things had been bad between us for a while, but didn't know just how bad or the real reason for our problems. I was very emotional, but at the same time Emma could see I was very angry. I kept telling her that the break-up wasn't Tracey's fault, but I couldn't give her the full explanation she deserved. It was just one of many bad days I had at the office around this time, and I knew Emma was worried about me and the way I was behaving. I think that once she knew about Tracey and me, she put some of my actions down to us splitting up and the constant stress of the business. Of course, the biggest factor was one that I had to keep hidden from her.

I'm not sure what Sophie and Libby thought about their parents finally splitting up. I hadn't really been living at the house for some time although I would try to see the girls as often as I could and would be there when Tracey was away working. I would stay at the house, but it wasn't really my home. The girls were growing up fast and I still wanted to be a big part of their lives. If there was one good thing to come out of me moving out of the house it was that neither of them had to put up with the angry words when Tracey and I had a row.

After my outburst at Tracey via text messages when I was in Portugal, we had calmed down a bit. She'd suggested that I spend Christmas Day with her, Sophie and Libby. The thought of us all being together and enjoying the day seemed like a nice idea and I agreed. I stayed at the house before Christmas as well, while she went off on a trip. I was happy to do it and was looking forward to spending time with the girls. But I did a silly thing. I looked in a bag belonging to Tracey and discovered a Christmas card she'd written to the man she had been seeing. Once again a tide of anger spread over me and I just flipped, but I wasn't just angry, I was really very sad as well. It all became a bit overwhelming.

One morning I was running late, Emma came to the house and I just keeled over and collapsed in front of her. Apparently, Sophie phoned for an ambulance and both of them were convinced that their father was having another heart attack. Emma stayed with me all night while they carried out tests and I was in a very emotional state. I kept telling Emma that I had issues but never told her what they were. They assured her that my collapse didn't have anything to do with my heart. I was discharged the next day and although Emma was relieved, she was more convinced than ever that there was something else wrong with her dad. She believed I was dying.

When Christmas Day arrived I wasn't sure I was doing the right thing. I wanted to be with the girls and with Tracey but at the same time I knew we couldn't really play happy families. There was too much going on. Once I had found that card in Tracey's bag I had sent texts to her and it was clear I wasn't pleased about it. I told her that I'd promised the kids that I would be over for Christmas, but after that I was going to walk out of her life. I also told her that I was sorry for all the hurt and pain that I might have caused her and I meant it. I had no idea I would cause even more hurt and pain on a day that was supposed to be a happy family occasion.

The whole idea of Tracey having another man in her life really upset me. I started to think that maybe it wasn't too late for me to halt things. Perhaps I could pull back from going down the road that would eventually lead to me transitioning. Of course it was ridiculous, but I don't think I was thinking straight. My thoughts were being driven by emotion. I decided to stop talking to all my transgender friends. I gathered up all my female clothes and locked them away. I even spoke to Linda and asked her if it would be possible to sell them all and told her that I wanted to go home for Christmas because I was going to try and work things out. As usual she was sympathetic and listened to what I had to say, but she said she'd seen other people do exactly what I was doing now and then repeated her belief that if this thing inside me was so strong it wasn't going to go away.

'You're not a transvestite, Kellie, you're a woman who was born into a man's body and that's different. All you want to be is female.' I knew she was right but I wanted to see if I could some-how pull back from the brink. The fact that I was thinking this way is probably an indication of just how muddled and mixed up I was. I wasn't thinking clearly and had been in a downward spiral for some weeks.

When Emma heard that I intended to spend the day with Tracey and the girls I think she became a little concerned and I'm not sure she thought it was a particularly good idea, given what had happened between Tracey and me and the fact that we were living apart. Emma and Rich were going to be visiting family and having Christmas lunch with Jackie. Emma suggested I had a key to their house so that if things did go wrong while I was with Tracey I could just get in my car and head back. I took the key but I was still optimistic about how things might go and drove over to the house on Christmas Eve. As soon as I got there my optimism began to disappear. Things just weren't the same.

There weren't any bitter words, but there seemed to be an invisible barrier between Tracey and me. Pretty soon it became clear that we were going through the motions. It all felt a bit awkward and strained. I went and put my bag in the spare room, sat on the bed and wondered what the hell I was doing. It didn't even feel normal to be there. I really did feel like a stranger in a place that I once called my home.

Christmas morning was friendly and there was a bit of laughter and some joking around, but it all seemed a bit manufactured. Things began to seem strained and tense to me or perhaps that was the way I felt. Maybe too much had gone on between Tracey and me for us to have any hope of having a normal Christmas. She had spent more than four years carrying my secret and to think I could just call a halt to what was going on inside me was not only naïve, it was stupid.

Sophie had a little job at one of the local pubs and she was due to work on Christmas Day at lunchtime, so we decided to go there and see her before going back to the house to eat. As soon as we got to the pub I ordered champagne, but when it came to paying for it I realised I'd left my credit cards back at the house. I asked Tracey if she had a card with her; she didn't and quickly reminded me that I'd stopped one of her cards only a few weeks before. I went off to get a card and then ordered more champagne.

Tracey took a call on her phone and I assumed it was from the new man in her life. Just the thought of it began to upset me and although she told me it was from a friend of ours, I didn't really believe her (I later found out she was telling me the truth). I was drinking too much champagne and drinking it too fast. I looked around the pub at other people laughing and joking, looking as though they didn't have a care in the world and I asked myself, why me? Was I the only person in the pub that day who had the sort of problems I had and, if so, why? The combination of the alcohol and my already emotional state was not good. Tracey and the girls left the pub but I was in the mood to carry on. Time seemed to go quickly for me, as it often does when you're drinking, but it was certainly dragging for Tracey and the girls back at the house.

I eventually returned in a nasty mood and took myself off to my room. I sat on the bed and thought about what had happened that day and about how stupid I had been to ever think I could patch things up with Tracey. The whole thing was ridiculous. I'd spent a lifetime trying to battle my gender dysphoria and just when I was getting to the point of finally owning up to who I really was and who I wanted to be, I had tried one last attempt to be the person I really wasn't and it had ended in disaster.

I sat there feeling more and more morose. Everything seemed such a mess. I had no fight left in me and I felt I couldn't go on. I began to swallow pills. Any pills I could find. I swallowed my heart pills, my blood pressure pills and some aspirin and paracetamol. I wanted to get the job done quickly. I was angry and sad, crying as I stuffed the tablets down my throat. I wanted to take enough to gently drift off and die, but then I began to think of what I was doing. I was going to kill myself in the house that Tracey and the girls shared.

My counsellor and I had once talked about people committing suicide and she had said that often people who do so in their own home have something against their partner or kids. That wasn't the case with me. I still loved Tracey and the girls. I didn't want them to have to live with the memory of me killing myself in the place that had been our family home. I decided I would get out of the house. I staggered downstairs, grabbed the leads for the two dogs and took them out with me. I didn't know where I was going, but just began walking, swallowing more pills as I wandered out of the front door and stumbled down the road. Everything seemed so strange and I began to feel lightheaded. I turned a corner and the dogs must have seen a cat or something in a block of flats we were passing and they lurched towards whatever it was, pulling me with them. I hadn't been prepared for the sudden movement and the next thing I remember was hearing the voice of a woman asking how I was. She must have recognised me because she was using my name as she spoke to me.

'Frank, Frank, are you okay? Can you hear me? Frank, Frank!' I could hear her voice but couldn't really focus on her face. By this time I could feel one of my dogs licking me and then I heard a man's voice saying he had called an ambulance.

'Just sit him up and keep him talking,' he was saying.

I slowly began to come round and said I didn't want an ambulance. They were concerned about the state I was in and asked if I was drunk and what had happened. I had no idea how long I'd been lying there before these two people found me. It was all a bit of a daze and I'd lost all sense of time. I eventually managed to get on all fours before clambering to my feet and pushing the couple out of the way. I wasn't being aggressive, I just wanted to get out of there before the ambulance arrived. They handed me the dogs' leads and I began to walk.

As I walked away I began to sob. What the hell had I done, was I mad? I'd left the house because I didn't want to die there, but now I realised I didn't really want to die at all. I walked for quite some time before getting back to the house. Sophie wasn't around and I tried to tell Tracey what I'd done, but I was still all over the place and we had a row. I think the way I was acting and talking really frightened her and she ran upstairs with Libby. I ran after them and found them both in Libby's room sitting on the bed. What followed was horrible as all hell broke loose in front of poor little Libby.

Her parents had yet another row and then she saw her dad completely lose it as I went mad and locked them in the room. I was still in a semi-daze and right on the edge. I went back to my room, threw myself on the bed and began crying. Sometime later I heard the front door open and then a little while after that I heard it close again. I staggered to my feet and came out of the room calling Tracey's name. I must have called it three or four times, but there was no reply. Tracey had gone and so had Libby.

Tracey later told me that she had to phone her friend because she was so terrified of what I might do next. The friend came to the house and unlocked Libby's door so that the two of them could get out. They'd run down the stairs and out of the house, slamming the door behind them. They spent the rest of the day with her friend, afraid to come home while I was still in the house.

I knew I had to get out and in my depressed state I began to swallow more pills, threw the dogs and my bag into the car and then got behind the wheel. Suicidal thoughts returned and I thought about writing the car off. There is a big gap in my memory as to what did happen and the next thing I remember is sitting in my car at Emma's house. How I got there I will never know. Perhaps somewhere in my brain I'd remembered her saying that if anything went wrong I should get back to her place and let myself in. The fact that I'd managed to get to her house in one piece was a miracle and it was all I could do to press her number on my mobile phone. I slurred and spluttered my words, but kept telling her that I'd ruined everyone's Christmas. I made the call at 7.00 pm and Emma told me she was on her way and not to do anything stupid.

By the time she arrived I was more upset and remorseful and said I'd let everyone down, including Emma, because I'd managed to spoil her day as well. I kept slurring my words and I had trouble focussing on anything she was saying to me. I managed to tell her I'd taken all sorts of tablets and drunk a lot of champagne. She got straight on to the NHS helpline to get some quick advice from them. Not surprisingly they said I should go straight to a hospital, but I told Emma that I wasn't going to do that. I knew that if I did I'd be all over the tabloid newspapers in the next few days.

Emma tried to make sure that I drank as much fluid as I could and kept talking to me. She didn't want me to drift off to sleep and knew that as long as I was talking and drinking, the effect of what I had taken would eventually start to wear off. She sat up all night, watching me breathe and talking to me, terrified that if she left me alone I wouldn't be alive in the morning. We talked about what I had tried to do and I told her that I'd come close to trying to end it all on a few occasions. She desperately wanted to know what was wrong with me, but all I would say was that I had 'issues'. It must have been pretty horrible for her to see me in that sort of state. She'd already seen how moody and depressed I was at the office and she'd also witnessed me collapsing. It was no wonder that she was concerned and had come to the conclusion that there was something seriously wrong. The more Emma saw of the way I was acting, the more she believed that her father was dying.

I will always be grateful to her for what she did that night. Her care and love for me was very special. I knew I was putting her through a lot of mental anguish, but just didn't feel I could tell her exactly what was wrong. She was my daughter, I was her dad. How could I tell her that I was transsexual and wanted to be female? It would shatter her life just as it had shattered Tracey's and the thought of it terrified me.

On Boxing Day I felt a lot better. Emma had nursed me through the worst of the effects and, after a shower, we sat and talked about what had happened. Emma once again asked what was wrong with me and why I'd acted the way I had, but I wouldn't give her a straight answer. I could see she was happy to have me with her so that she could keep an eye on me and I had a relaxed day and felt really calm. We went to the cinema, had a meal at the house in the evening and I began to feel a lot better about myself. The cloud of depression had lifted, but I knew from experience that it could return at any time. I was determined to try and stay upbeat.

The next day I told Emma that I was going to ask James, Carla and Mark – who worked in my office – to come over and suggested we all go to the pub in the evening. We hadn't had a proper office party so I decided we'd celebrate Christmas belatedly. James couldn't make it but Mark and Carla did and we had a really happy evening. We drank champagne as if it was going out of fashion but this time I was in a much better frame of mind. I was happy and I wanted everyone around me to be the same. It was nice to see Emma and Rich laughing and joking after what I'd put them through and it was just the sort of uplifting evening I needed. For a few hours I felt good. In fact, it felt so good that I suggested we did the same again the next night.

The champagne started flowing once again and there was lots of laughing and joking going on. I felt really happy and con-

Emma and me on her wedding day in 2011.

Me and my friend Ray at my 60th birthday party.

One of the last pictures of Frank, growing my hair out at my mum's 81st birthday party (*top left*). The last picture before Spanish surgery (*above*). Here I am at the Bloomsbury Hair Clinic, having my hairpiece attached in February 2015 (*left*).

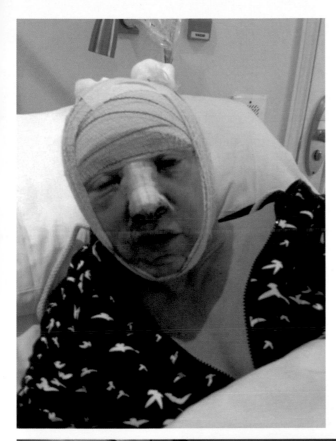

Straight after my Spanish surgery in December 2013 (*left*). I join my family after surgery to celebrate my 61st birthday in what is possibly the last picture of me as Frank (*below*).

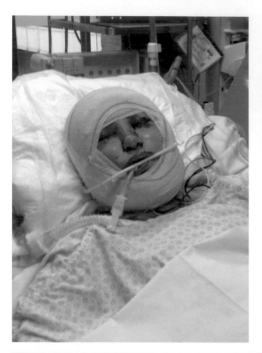

I recover following surgery in Belgium.

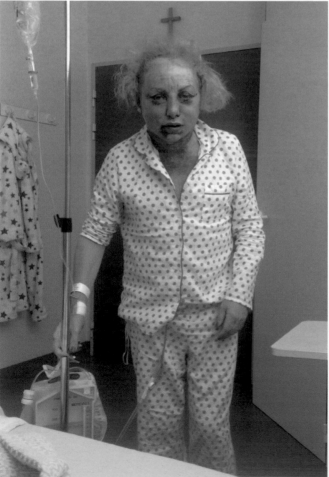

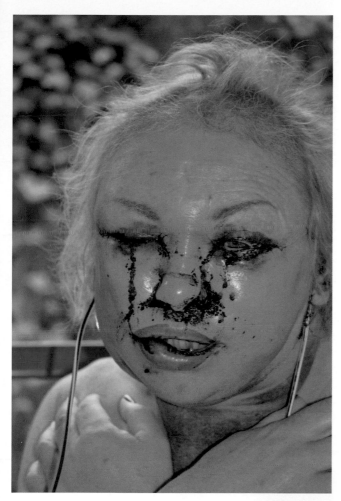

The morning after surgery in Belgium (*top*)
before I returned home (*right*).

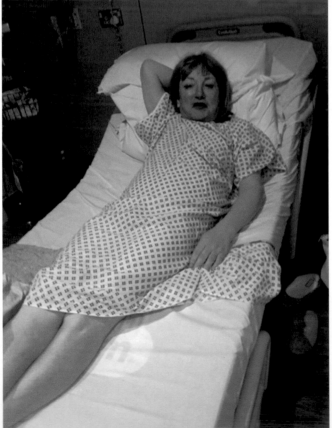

Me and Nick, a friend from the TG Pals support group (*above*). I prepare for my last round of surgery (*left*).

I relax with my family at a dinner thanking them for their support (*top*) and relax in Portugal following my first facial surgery in December 2013 (*left*).

Me and my daughter Libby (wearing one of my wigs!) (*above*). Me and Dee (*right*). I relax with my dogs in Portugal in January 2015 (*below*).

tented, but then everything changed. I tried to stay happy, tried to make people believe that everything was fine, but it wasn't. I realised that all I was really doing was putting on another Frank Maloney act, just as I had my whole life. I looked at Emma and as much as I loved her, I'd stopped myself from telling her what was really wrong with me. I was lying to her and she didn't deserve that. I suddenly felt very sad and the depression began to close in on me. Emma could see the sudden sadness in my eyes. She knew me inside out. Knew when her dad was happy or sad and knew when I was feeling troubled. She suggested that we go outside for some fresh air and as we walked out of the pub I began to cry. She asked me what was wrong, but I didn't really say anything, just mumbled something through the tears. She put her arms around me and gave me a cuddle.

'What is it, Dad, what's the matter?' she asked and I could see the anxiety in her face. She was really worried and I'm sure she expected me to finally tell her what she'd suspected, that I had an illness and was dying.

'Please, Dad,' I heard her say, 'just tell me.'

Without really thinking I told her, but as I did it I couldn't face her. I couldn't look at my own daughter. Instead I looked away from her as I blurted out exactly what had been troubling me for my entire life. 'I'm not normal, Emms,' I said as tears ran down my cheeks. 'I'm transgender. I was born with the wrong body, I should have been a girl.'

I told her that I'd been like it all of my life and that I'd been battling against my feelings all that time. I explained that I'd gone to Tracey's for Christmas because even at this stage I was still trying to cling to the hope that I could somehow manage things. To live the normal life everyone expected of me, but it had just become too hard and too difficult. I could tell what I'd said had shocked her. What daughter wouldn't be shocked when her father tells her he wants to be a woman and had felt as though he should have been a female for his entire life? There were a few moments of silence, but then Emma wiped her own eyes and smiled at me. It was such a beautiful smile, full of sympathy and understanding.

'Don't worry about it, Dad,' she told me. 'I'll always be here for you.'

Those words meant so much to me, and from that moment I instantly felt there was a real bond between us. I had shared my secret with my oldest daughter. I could see I had stunned her and who knows what was going on in her mind? What I do know is that she showed me nothing but love and compassion as we tried to dry our eyes before going back into the pub. I knew she must have had dozens of questions she wanted to ask me and have answered. I knew I had to ask Emma to carry the same sort of burden as Tracey had. Emma knew my secret and I knew that it now had to become hers as well.

CHAPTER FIFTEEN

Paying the price

I couldn't get to sleep that night after I told my daughter what was really going on with me. I went over what had happened and what it now meant. It was a relief to finally tell Emma, but I wondered just how devastated she must have felt when she'd found out. She had been worried about me for some time but I knew for certain that none of her worries would have involved her dad being transgender. At about four in the morning I went down to the kitchen still feeling restless and decided to have some tea. Not long after Emma appeared and we sat and chatted. I knew she had all sorts of questions she wanted to ask and there was a lot I wanted to tell her.

I tried to explain to her the mental pain I'd been suffering all of my life, how I had tried to battle through and beat the urges I had, but how I now felt those urges had won, and mentioned that I felt a big moment for me was the death of my dad. After that, I think the real fight in me ended. There had been moments where I still thought I could beat it, and that was one of the reasons for having Christmas with Tracey, but the reality was that I knew things were only going to go one way from now on.

She was confused and probably still in shock, but she listened and tried to take it all in. It felt very strange in one way but incredibly reassuring in another. I knew that confiding in her had been the right thing to do, but it was going to be difficult for both of us, particularly her. She had to try and get her head around what I had told her and I knew that she would have to speak to Rich and realised that his support was going to be vital to her.

Emma was relieved to know what had been wrong with me, but I could tell she was still concerned and one of the things she suggested was me moving closer to her, to a small house near her that she still owned. I could move all of my female stuff in there, nobody would trouble me and there was a small garden for the dogs. I had to admit that it seemed like a really good idea. Emma was still working with me at the office and it was reassuring to know she would be just around the corner if ever I needed her. The house would give me the privacy and independence I needed.

Emma suggested a few days later that I should make a list of the people to tell. I realised I would also have to tell Sophie and Libby at some stage, but the person I knew I had to speak to next was my mother. Both my mother and father had always been very important to me. It had been horrible seeing them split up all those years ago, but it never changed my love for them and I was happy that they had both been able to enjoy some of the success I'd had with my boxing career. My mum loved boxing and would always be at any promotion I was involved with, whether it was in Britain or abroad. She used to love her trips to America to watch the Lennox Lewis fights and she genuinely enjoyed boxing and lots of other sports as well.

Although I loved my mother I knew that there had always been a barrier between us and that barrier had been put there by me. It was all part of the safety mechanism I'd constructed in order to protect myself and project the image I wanted to convey. I was never really that affectionate, it was as though I was holding back, because I was too afraid to let my emotions go. As a kid I had been very affectionate towards her, but that gradually began to disappear as the adult Frank Maloney began to emerge. We always got on, I would see her on a regular basis and I always tried to look after her, but there was a certain distance and it was all down to me.

I asked my mother if we could meet at my old house, the one that no longer felt like home, but which Tracey and the girls still lived in. I was nervous and wasn't sure how I would tell her or what I would say. How do you tell your mother that the son she had brought into the world now wanted to be her daughter? It wasn't something I was looking forward to. When my mum arrived we sat chatting for a while and drinking tea, but then I knew I couldn't put the moment off any longer.

'Mum,' I said, 'I've got something to tell you.' As I said the words I put my arms around her and gently began to cry. 'I'm not the person you think I am. I'm transsexual. I was born into the wrong body and I've wanted to be a girl for as long as I can remember.' It was really difficult telling her but in an instant all my worries and anxiety disappeared. She looked at me and now we both had tears running down our faces.

'Well, is that all?' she said. 'We'll just have to change the "i" in your name to an "e".' She tried to reassure me with a smile and a hug, telling me that I should have told her a long time ago. 'You're mine,' she added. 'I brought you into this world and while I'm alive, I'll always love you.'

Once again I felt tremendous relief, just as I had with Emma. It was a very emotional moment for both of us and it allowed me to show my true feelings towards her, something I probably hadn't done since I was a child. It had taken that long, but now at least she could start to understand what had been going on with me and I think a lot more of what had gone on in the past began to fall into place for her. She has since told me that on a lot of occasions when I visited her, she would notice that I had sad eyes and often seemed distracted. She put it down to the pressure of my work, which was partly true, but she also believes it was because I just wasn't able to tell her how troubled I was.

'Mum,' I said. 'How could I have told you when you think of the environment I was brought up in? And what do you think dad would have thought of me? You might have been able to accept things, but it would have been so hard for him and I don't think he would have been able to cope with it.'

She understood exactly what I meant and didn't really have to say anything. Instead, she just gave me the biggest cuddle I think I'd ever had from her. We looked at each other crying and laughing at the same time and I felt a closeness to her the like of which I'd never felt before. Having spent more than four years with Tracey as the only member of my family who knew the secret I'd been keeping all of my life, I had now included Emma and my mum. A few weeks ago I'd have been terrified at the thought of them knowing. Now all I felt was relief.

They had been understanding and sympathetic, which had made telling them so much easier. Yet, having been so certain about who I really was when I spoke to my mother, I then allowed my thinking process to become muddled once again. It was as if despite everything, the Frank in me just wouldn't let go.

Emma and I had chatted to a couple of woman in the pub over Christmas and I had ended the night exchanging phone numbers with one. She was a management accountant and was going through a divorce. I found it easy to talk with her and we got on well. It wasn't long before the two of us were seeing quite a bit of each other. We'd go for meals and go to the cinema. Sometimes I'd go over to her place in the evening and other times she would come over to me, but there was nothing sexual in our relationship. I certainly didn't do it as part of my cover to protect myself. I liked her and enjoyed being in her company. It must have been confusing for Emma. There I was telling her that I wanted to be a woman and then she saw me going out with a girl.

She did tell me not to rush into anything, but once again I started thinking that maybe it wasn't too late. Maybe I could pull back. Maybe I could end up having a relationship with this woman. I even went to the warehouse where I'd been keeping all of my female clothes with the intention of burning them and getting rid of everything. It was as if I thought that by disposing of the clothes I would dispose of the way I really felt, which of course was ridiculous.

When I got to the warehouse and looked at everything I just couldn't get rid of the female wardrobe I'd painstakingly built up. I ended up putting everything into my car and taking the stuff back to my house. I just couldn't do it. I didn't want to get rid of things that clearly meant so much to me. If ever there was an indication of what my true feelings were, that was surely it, but I still had the ability to delude myself. I was a 60-year-old man who had been taking hormones for the past two months but I still continued to play the Frank Maloney role for large chunks of my life.

In one sense, I had to be Frank because I still had a business to run. I'd had a tough year, but David Price's career was going well and I was getting a buzz from watching him make the sort of progress I hoped would one day lead to a world heavyweight title fight. In October 2012, Price had won against Audley Harrison with a first round victory in a contest for which the hype and publicity had started the previous summer.

It was the year of the London Olympics and both men had won medals at previous Olympics when they were amateurs, David got a bronze in Beijing and Audley claimed gold at Sydney, so it made sense to start the publicity wagon rolling on the back of the Games being held in the UK. I could see the sense in this and was happy to do the usual round of press conferences and television interviews. One TV slot came on the same day I made my first visit to the transgender clinic.

I'd been a bit nervous about going to the clinic on my own and asked Jan if she would go along with me. I wanted her to give me an opinion of the doctor I was due to see. It was the first time Jan had seen me dressed as Kellie and, although it was a relatively little thing, I was pleased that she'd finally seen me in my female mode. The consultation went well, Jan said she thought the doctor was fine and I came out of the clinic in a happy mood. The rain was pouring down as we made our way to my little Mini and I told Jan that I was going to have to change for the interview. As I began to take my shoes, tights, hairpiece and dress off in the confines of my small car, the windows began to mist up as the rain continued to fall down. So there we were, in the front of the car with me wriggling all over the place trying to get my female clothes off and my male clothes on. If anyone had caught sight of us I don't know what they would have thought.

I dropped Jan off at the station while still wearing my false breasts and realised I also had to get rid of my make-up as well. I remembered that there was a big garage in Battersea that I'd been to before which had a toilet. I must have been in there for ages making sure I got every trace of make-up off until I felt it was safe for me to get back in my car and head for the studios. What a crazy few hours it had been. One minute I was in a private transgender clinic in the West End, telling a doctor that I wanted to be a woman, and then a couple of hours later I was in a television studio telling everyone that David Price is going to be a future world heavyweight champion. What a strange life I was living.

By January 2013, Price had amassed an unbeaten record of 15 fights and was about to go into his biggest contest, against an American named Tony Thompson in Liverpool. Price was expected to cement his place at the top table of heavyweight boxing by winning and moving on to a world title elimination fight. On paper he looked like a clear favourite but as the old saying goes, fights are won in the ring and not on paper.

Poor David got caught in the second round and any hopes of getting the eliminator in his next fight were shattered by the punch Thompson caught him with. I immediately got the TV people to show me a replay over and over again of what had happened. I noticed that David had been caught behind the ear and knew this was something I was going to play up at the post-fight press conference and in interviews. The line I used was that the blow had disorientated Price.

After the press, I went back to the arena to meet with family and friends. As I walked, I was talking about the fight and began to explain that if only David could have managed to go down on one knee and take a count of eight, things might have been different. I demonstrated what I meant, bending down and it was then that my body felt very strange and I began to collapse. There was a lot of commotion and I could hear voices but not very clearly. I didn't really know where I was or what had happened but I had a blurred vision of my mum and Sophie running over to me. I suddenly heard Sophie's voice.

'Look at me, Dad,' I heard her say, but I don't think I could focus properly. 'Look at me!' I heard her shout again.

I didn't fully come round until I was in the back of an ambulance. I could now hear both Emma and Sophie trying to talk to me. Emma was saying that I had to go to the hospital and I think I must have started protesting, because the next voice I heard was Sophie's and she was clearly upset. 'If you don't go to the hospital, Dad, I'll never talk to you again,' she yelled. Poor Sophie must have been really worried. She had been at the house with Emma the day I'd last passed out and she had called the ambulance. This time around, my blood pressure was high. They wheeled me into a hospital and some guy recognised me and managed to give me the benefit of some typical scouse wit.

'Thought it was Pricey who got knocked out tonight, Frank, not you!' he joked. Despite what had happened, it actually made me smile.

The doctors wanted to keep me in overnight for observation. Emma was with me all through the night and I could see she was worried. I began to feel depressed while I was lying there. It wasn't just the fact that David had lost, it was more to do with the confusion I felt. I thought I had started to get my life in order, but it still seemed as chaotic as ever. As I drifted off to sleep that night I began to wonder why I was bothering to put myself through all the stress that a big fight caused me. I also began to wonder if this might be the right time to walk away from it all. I liked David Price and I wanted him to succeed. He'd suffered a bad defeat, but that could happen in boxing. If I walked away now, was I taking the easy way out, and did I want to end my career on a losing note? If he wanted me to help him come back from the loss and try to re-build his career I knew I could do it. Whatever I decided, I knew I had some thinking to do and some big decisions to make once I got out of hospital.

Happily, the doctors discharged me the next day. There had been nothing wrong with my heart, which was obviously the major concern given my history and they seemed to think it might have all been caused by my poor diet in the week leading up to the fight, when I'd lived off chocolate and endless cups of tea.

I really did need to sort myself out and decide what I was going to do with my life. I couldn't keep switching between Frank and Kellie, hoping to keep both alive and happy. It just wasn't possible. I'd taken the woman I'd met in the pub to the fight in Liverpool, but really I knew the relationship with her was going nowhere. How could it? She was very nice and we got on, but there was no point in me kidding myself that there was going to be any future. I needed to get my head straight and instead of changing my mind all the time, I had to make sure I was going to be true to myself.

Emma had started to play a big role in my life. Now that she knew all about me it was easier to talk and ask her opinion. We would talk while walking the dogs and it was so reassuring for me to have her help and support. Having a transgender father was still very new to her and I realised that she needed to keep asking questions and finding out more about the way I felt. This had all happened so quickly for her but she was kind and always willing to help. I know she spoke to Tracey and my mum about me and I think they all found it a help to be able to talk to another member of the family about someone they all loved and cared for.

For Tracey it must have been a huge relief. She'd had to keep my secret from the family and at times it wasn't very pleasant for her. She had bad moments when Sophie had pretty much blamed her for me looking so unhappy and being so emotional, and Emma had also asked her what had been wrong. Poor Tracey wouldn't say a word. I'd asked her not to say anything and she was determined to keep my secret. At least now there was my mum and Emma too but I'd made them swear they wouldn't say anything and I knew how tough that was on them.

I had a meeting with David, his lawyer and his trainer to discuss the way forward. They were determined that they wanted me to get him a re-match with Thompson which I was very much against. I felt we could get to where we wanted to be by going around Thompson. I'd never liked the idea of instant re-matches – sometimes it's a case of a boxer coming up against someone whose style just doesn't suit them. I thought David was a better fighter than Thompson but I didn't think he needed to take the risk of an immediate return. In the past I would have dug my heels in and argued the point, but I just didn't have the fight in me. I said that I would do what they wanted and try to get the re-match.

I came away wondering if I really had the appetite to carry on in the boxing business. I felt worn down and worn out by it. I knew my life was going to change and I wasn't sure there would be any room for boxing in it. I did what I said I would try to do and got David the re-match he wanted. In the months leading up to the July promotion, I knew I was falling out of love with the sport that had been so much a part of my life since the age of 11. I talked to Emma about the way I felt and the more I thought about it, the more I began to believe that this would be my last promotion.

I was still seeing Jan – she was really a life counsellor – but a transsexual friend suggested it might be useful to me to see a counsellor who was herself transgender and I found one who had transitioned from male to female. I went to see her dressed in my male clothes but gave my name as Kellie. As soon as I walked into her consulting room I was stunned when she said, 'I know who you are.' Then she gave me another surprise by saying she'd boxed as an amateur when she was young.

After the surprises we began to talk and it was really interesting for me to speak to someone like her. There are so many emotional issues involved in transitioning, not just in the way you feel about yourself, but also the worries you have about what it might do to your family and how it will affect them. I knew that living as a woman after so many years living as a man was going to be strange and at times difficult. We talked about how different it is being a woman and that you are not treated in the same way as a man is, even when it comes to very simple things like buying a coffee. I had to agree with her, because there had been a definite difference when I'd been out in public as Kellie.

It was a strange situation as I prepared for the David Price rematch. I don't think I'd ever felt like it in the build-up to a big fight – I was right at the centre of the promotion in Liverpool, yet I felt detached. I did all that I should do, but in the week leading up to the contest I didn't want to stay in the fight hotel. Instead I rented a houseboat and stayed on it with Emma. I had to smile when I saw the name –*Titanic*. I didn't go out at night or spend a lot of time with the press and others in the business. I was happier wandering around the shops with Emma and looking at the female clothes in the different stores.

The one thing I did do was go over the top at the press conferences. The showman in me just couldn't help it because in my heart of hearts I knew this was probably going to be my last fight. Win, lose or draw my mind was made up. I couldn't push myself as I once had and my path towards transitioning seemed much clearer. I may have taken a few detours along the way, but I knew what I really wanted to do and that was to pack Frank Maloney away forever.

I would have loved to have gone out on a winning note, not just for me but for David. I was desperate for him to win. He was a really nice kid and I know how keen he was to avenge the defeat he'd suffered against Thompson five months earlier. But it wasn't to be. Price actually had Thompson down in the second round, but the American managed to recover and the pattern of the fight changed completely. I think Thompson's recovery drained confidence from Price. He had to try and get rid of his opponent all over again, but he was never able to. The American won in the fifth round.

As usual, I was asked to do a post-fight interview. I sat on the ring apron answering questions and trying to put a brave face on matters but as the interview came to an end my brave face disappeared and I began to cry. The guy interviewing me didn't really know what to do. It wasn't what boxing people expected from Frank Maloney. The mask I'd hidden behind for all those years had slipped. It was very emotional because as I left the arena that night I was probably saying goodbye to boxing, but it was more than that. I think I was also beginning to embrace what was to come. There really was no turning back now I had a new life to lead.

A few days later I was back at the transgender clinic fully dressed as a woman, bending over in the doctor's surgery with my knickers and tights around my ankles as he gave me an injection to lower my testosterone levels. Exactly one week after the disappointment in Liverpool I was back in the north of England – but this time it was to attend Sparkle, a weekend festival for the transgender community which was held in Manchester. It was so nice after all the stresses and strains I'd been through to be able to go away with friends for the weekend and be myself, be Kellie.

I was able to relax and enjoy myself, although there was one in-cident which I could have done without. I was out at a club one night with some other girls and as I walked across the floor a guy stuck his hand up my dress. I swivelled around as quick as a flash and hit him right across the face and told him in no uncertain terms never to try anything like that with me. I might have been on the road to transitioning and becoming Kellie full time, but I was quite happy that the old Frank was still around for moments like that. Mind you, I did spend the rest of the evening with my back against the wall!

I'd had enough of trying to lead two lives and decided that the next few months were going to be about being honest with myself, being honest with others and continuing with what I now knew I had to do, which was fully transition. One of the people I knew I had to be honest with was my brother Vince. He lived in Australia with his family, but came over in the summer when we had a party for my mum's birthday. I'd spoken to my mum about telling him and said that I didn't want to say anything to Eugene yet. I had the feeling that Eugene's reaction would not be good and told her she could tell him at some stage in the future but that this wasn't the right time.

It had been a long time since Vince had shared that flat in Islington with me and Alan. We didn't see that much of each oth-er, but we kept in touch. I knew that I couldn't let him go back to Australia without telling him about myself but wasn't sure how I would do it. We went out for a family meal while he was over and just as he was leaving I told him I wanted to take him out later that week because I had something I wanted to tell him. I decided that Emma and I would take him for a Chinese meal. The restaurant was near my old house and I usually felt comfortable, but that night I couldn't help but feel a little bit on edge. Here I was, about to tell my youngest brother that he was soon going to have an older sister. It wasn't going to be easy but it had to be done.

'Vince,' I said, 'I've got something to tell you.' I looked at Emma and she gave me a nod of encouragement. I cleared my throat. 'I don't know how you're going to take this, but I had to tell you face-to-face. Vince, I'm a transsexual.'

He looked at me wide-eyed and clearly stunned. I knew I had to give him a few seconds for what I had said to sink in but then I continued before he had a chance to say anything. 'I'm going to change the way I live and I'm going to change my body to the way I think it always should have been,' I added. 'All my life I've been fighting with myself and now it's time to stop.' I told him that I'd had all sorts of counselling over a long period of time but this thing wasn't going to go away. It was really now about me accepting who I was and making a new life for myself.

'What sort of counselling have you had?' Vince asked. 'You haven't had the right sort of counselling. I could get you a counsellor.' I knew Vince had very strong Christian beliefs and that he lived his life by the Bible. I had no problem with that but I felt put out by his reaction.

'Vince, I'm not going to argue with you, but if you've got someone who can stop me feeling the way I do then they could earn an absolute fortune. This is not about choice. For years I fought it. I always wanted to be the perfect male, but I was also very unhappy with myself and I don't want to be like that anymore.'

I think Vince began to realise just how difficult my life had been and the way in which I had needed to keep everything from the world for so long. I could see there were tears welling up in his eyes and there were tears in mine as well. I quickly grabbed a napkin to try and brush them away from my face. For some reason I didn't want him to see me cry.

I explained that I had started the process that would end in me becoming a woman. I was taking hormones and that my body would be slowly changing. I also told him that I was probably going to retire from the boxing business because I didn't see how I could carry on with all that was going to be happening in my private life. I knew it was a lot for Vince to have to take on board. All his life I had been his oldest brother, I'd taken him with me and looked after him when our parents had split up. He'd seen me make a successful career in one of the most macho environments in the sporting world and now I was telling him I wanted to become a woman. For a few seconds I wondered exactly what he was going to say. Then he looked at me and spoke.

'You've got to do what makes you happy,' he told me. 'No matter what happens I'll always love you and you'll always be my brother.'

It was really good to hear those words. I knew he must be shocked and confused. It was only natural that he would be, but once again when I'd shared my secret with a member of my family, the response had been good. I joked with him that it might not be long before I was his sister but knew Vince still had a lot to take in and it wasn't going to be easy.

A day or two later I spoke to my mum and asked her what Vince had said after I'd told him. She mentioned that Vince still felt I hadn't been getting the right counselling. It annoyed me, but then I suppose with his religious beliefs and the shock of finding out about me, he was bound to search for reasons just as lots of other people would. The simple fact of the matter was that I didn't really have any control over the way I felt. All I was doing was going along with my inner feelings rather than fighting a constant battle with them. If I could stop what was now going on in my life I would. If there was a pill that prevented me from wanting to become a woman I'd take it, and so would other transsexuals. We don't choose to be born in the wrong body with the wrong gender and the process of trying to correct what went wrong at birth is not easy. Apart from the hormones I was on at the time, I'd also started an often painful electrolysis treatment to remove hairs. My emotions were continually up and down, I'd lost my marriage and I might lose my two youngest daughters when I broke the news to them.

I took Vince to the airport and told him on the way just how much I appreciated his support and he mentioned that when we'd lived in the flat together he did think there was something a bit different about me, but never really wanted to bring the subject up. I joked with him that I'd heard my gender dysphoria was hereditary and we laughed. Just before he went through to catch his plane we hugged and I couldn't stop the tears welling up. Vince told me to stop crying and said once again that he'd always be there for me. I knew he meant it and also knew it was probably going to be the last time my brother saw Frank Maloney.

A couple of weeks later, I flew out to Portugal and took another giant step when my mum met Kellie for the first time. Since the moment I had told her about myself I'd felt so much closer to her than I ever had before. Her reaction and love had been so important to me and at the age of 80 she'd shown the sort of understanding and compassion that marked her out as a very special person. It was lovely having my mum with me and talking about all sorts of things. Nothing specific, just odd silly things, but at the same time they were the sort of conversations I'd never had before.

When she first saw me dressed fully as a woman we were going to go out for a meal. I went to my bedroom and spent quite a long time getting ready. I wanted to look good and also wanted to make sure my mother genuinely saw me as a woman and not as her son dressed up as a female. When I came out of my bedroom and stood in front of her, she smiled, looked at me and then said something that made me relax and laugh at the same time. 'I think you've got a bit too much make-up on, young lady!'

I took her advice and toned it down a bit before going out for the meal. I spent two days fully dressed as Kellie and we had a really good time together. Having her there and seeing her acceptance meant so much and the whole experience was also therapeutic. When I took her to the airport and kissed her good-bye I wanted to cry. I got back to the house and felt very alone. Mum's presence had filled the house for the past ten days and we'd had such a good time together and now I quickly began to feel depressed. My mood swings were definitely becoming more frequent and they could also be more severe at times, as I went over what was happening with my life and how it would be for me in the future.

Emma phoned and could tell I was feeling really down. She said she was going to book a flight and come out to see me. My mood changed almost immediately. The thought of her coming out to see me lifted my spirits. Emma had taken an awful lot on board since she found out about me. I knew it wasn't easy for her and it must have been taking its toll, but she never said anything. She just continued to give me her love, help and support. I met her at the airport dressed as Frank. She still hadn't seen me in my female mode and that was another bridge I knew I was going to have to cross in the future. She did manage to get a glimpse of Kellie because I turned up still wearing pink toenail varnish which I'd forgotten to get rid of!

Sophie and Libby also came out during my time there and Libby became very curious about some of the female clothes in the wardrobe of the bedroom that Tracey and I had always used. 'These are not mum's clothes,' she said prancing around in some of the stuff I'd been wearing only a matter of days ago.

'No,' I admitted, trying to buy myself some time and then said they belonged to a lady friend I'd had staying with me for a few days. I don't know if she believed me. The only thing I am certain of is that the truth would have seemed too far-fetched for Libby to consider it.

It was going to be hard to walk away from boxing. I'd been bound up in it for so long and the people and characters in it had become part of the fabric of my life. One of those was a guy called Dean Powell. He'd worked for me as a trainer and match-maker over the years and was very much part of the UK boxing scene. Towards the end of my holiday I got some devastating news about him. Linda had flown out to spend some time with me and once again I felt very relaxed and happy because I could be Kellie. Be myself. I was sitting in my car waiting for her when I got a call from a boxing colleague.

'Frank, are you sitting down?' this guy asked.

'Yes, why, what's happened?'

'Dean Powell is dead.'

I couldn't believe it. I'd been speaking to Dean only a couple of days before. We'd talked a lot about boxing. About the way the sport was going and the fact that I was seriously think-ing of walking away from it. We were both moaning and groan-ing. Dean didn't sound particularly happy but he didn't sound suicidal either and yet that was apparently exactly what he was just days later. On a September morning in London, poor Dean had thrown himself under a train at New Cross Gate. I was shocked and had trouble trying to take it all in. Then I started to think of why it might have happened. What sort of pressure and unhappiness drives someone to actually want to kill themselves? It was horrible. Dean was such a nice guy and very easy going. I would shout and scream at him sometimes when he worked for me, but he knew that was just the way I was and it never stopped us from being friends, or having a long working relationship. Now he was gone. Whatever demons he'd had finally got the better of him and they had driven him to end his own life. It was tragic and very sad. Hearing about the death of someone you know well always is, but it also made me think about my own life.

I'd tried to take my own life and, luckily for me, had made a complete mess of it. I continued to have moments when I felt very down and depressed. I knew it was going to be difficult for me, but I knew there would be life after Frank. That Kellie was quite capable of having that life if I was committed enough to see things through. I sat down and began to list the pluses and minuses of being Frank and of being Kellie. When I looked at the sheet of paper it only confirmed what I already thought. I was happier being Kellie. Within a few weeks of returning from Portugal I released a press statement saying that I was retiring from boxing.

I immediately felt more at ease and happy. I took myself out of the public eye and pretty much disappeared from view. I refused countless requests for interviews and started to become a very private person. Once I'd made my decision everything became a lot clearer for me and I was able to focus on moving towards transitioning. It was exciting to think that I had a whole new world ahead of me but at the same time I was scared. I couldn't help it, because no matter how much I talked about it with Emma, my counsellors or other people from the transgender community, the thought of what I was going to do frightened me at times. I was going into the unknown.

The biggest fear I had at this time was the reaction of Sophie and Libby. What were they going to think? What would they do? What would they say? Would they still want me in their lives? Would they think I was a freak? Would they be sickened by their own father? There were so many different thoughts and in my darkest moments I would be very unhappy, often crying myself to sleep. I was very emotional and the mood swings seemed to become more severe.

It wasn't all doom and gloom. I would have lots of days when I was very happy and contented. It was a relief to finally be able to dress more as Kellie and I think that had a good effect on me. I also enjoyed socialising with the new friends I'd made and in October I attended a TransLiving weekend. Weekends like this were a real help to me and they involved people from right across the trans community. On this particular occasion after a few glasses of wine I was persuaded to enter the Miss TransLiving Golden competition and managed to win it. I had lots of photographs taken but asked the organisers not to publish them in their magazine. I was becoming more paranoid over the thought of being exposed in the press. It was a big fear. I knew I couldn't keep things secret for ever but I didn't want anything to happen yet. There was still so much to do and I wanted to be able to get on with it quietly and at my own pace. Going to weekends like this meant a lot to me.

I asked Emma if she would like to come with me to the next one. I knew she probably had mixed feelings, but she agreed. I think she wanted to know more about transsexuals and talk to people who had gone through the things I was now experiencing. Everything was so different for her now. Some of it was strange and upsetting, but there were funny moments too, like the time at the end of October when I went out shopping with her. With the next TransLiving weekend scheduled for November, both Emma and I ended up looking at dresses we might want to wear for the occasion. Yes, it was strange in one sense, but it was also funny and the good thing was that we were able to laugh about it.

I planned to undergo facial feminisation surgery at a clinic in Spain that December and then spend the festive holiday at the house in Portugal. Emma had helped me book everything including a villa to stay in while I was out there. She was going to come with me and Rich was going to be coming out for a time. He had been brilliant with everything and although I knew he'd been told what was going on by Emma, the two of us went for a while without really talking about it. When we were out walking the dogs one day I just began talking in a very matter-of-fact way and said how grateful I was for all that he and Emma were doing for me. I found it easy to talk to Rich. He'd been very understanding and while Emma bore the brunt of supporting me, I knew that he was probably doing the same for her and I was pleased she had him as her husband.

None of this was easy for my family. I knew that I wasn't going to have a brain transplant and that it was my body which was going to be modified. The difference was that I'd lived my whole life knowing that I was a female wrapped in a man's body. They knew nothing about how I felt. I gave them Frank Maloney and that was the person they had come to know. Now that was all going to change and I knew they would need time to try and come to terms with it.

I also knew the time was fast approaching when I would have to let Sophie and Libby know. I planned to do it before going to

Spain. Both of them had a right to know what was happening in their dad's life and why for so much of theirs they'd had to put up with my moods, anger and often erratic behaviour. I'd decided to tell Sophie first and arranged to take her out for a meal along with Emma. When we got to the restaurant the last thing I felt like was eating a three-course meal and I'm sure Emma felt the same, but I didn't want to just dive in and blurt everything out to Sophie. I'd told her there was something I needed to tell her and I suspect that like Emma, she thought I was going to say there was something medically wrong with me.

After we'd eaten the three of us found a quiet corner in the bar. I took both her hands in mine and looked at Sophie. She could see I was beginning to cry and slowly the tears came and rolled gently down my face. For what seemed like an absolute age I squeezed her hands tightly and then began to tell her. As the words came out of my mouth the look of shock and horror on Sophie's face was heart-breaking. She too began to cry and I walked her out of the bar so that we could carry on talking, just the two of us. Emma could see how upset Sophie was and she knew that after being hit by the shock wave of what I had told, she needed to be alone with her dad.

I can't really remember what I said to Sophie when we were alone. I remember her being so upset and hurt. Once again the tremendous feeling of guilt hit. I knew I'd detonated an emotional bomb that could destroy my own daughter. Sophie had walked into the restaurant as a bright, bubbly, carefree 18-year-old girl. She was going to be leaving it feeling con-fused, angry, sad and perhaps betrayed. I asked Emma if she would look after Sophie for me. I felt I had to get out and get some fresh air. I loved Sophie so much and wanted her in my life. I didn't want to lose her and we had always had a great relationship, but that night I honestly wondered if I had destroyed what we had forever.

CHAPTER SIXTEEN

Daddy's little secret

I'd made the decision to take myself out of public life to start living the way I knew I wanted to live, but at the same time I just couldn't help beating myself up. One minute I thought I was finding inner peace and coming to terms with the course of action I was going to take and then the next minute I felt as though I was losing everything.

Was I being selfish? Just doing what was right for me and not bothering about the consequences for others or was this whole thing just unstoppable, something that was carrying me along with it? I kept telling myself that I was still the same person, that I was just changing the wrapping and I truly believed that to be the case, but it didn't make things any easier. I had terrible bouts of depression and found myself bursting into tears for no apparent reason. Emma had been my rock and I don't know what I would have done without her.

After telling Tracey, Emma had been only the second person in my family I had confided in. She was losing her dad or at least the dad she had always known. Frank was going to disappear and Kellie was going to emerge. It was such a big thing for any daughter to take in, yet she had shown me nothing but love, understanding and support. I knew I was blessed to have her there beside me. She had lived with my secret for the past 11 months and she had been there when I broke the news to Sophie. The look of confusion and bewilderment in Sophie's face is something I will never forget and I knew she was still desperately trying to come to terms with what was happening. It was still early days for Sophie and I wasn't sure what she was thinking or if she was capable of understanding the way I felt and why I had no real control over my feelings and emotions. I knew how difficult it was for her and I could only guess at what was going on in her head now she realised her dad wanted to live the rest of his life as a woman. Both Emma and Sophie now knew what was going on and what I intended to do. Now it was time for me to finally break the news to little Libby.

I was dreading the thought of it but at the same time I knew I had to do it. I'd told Sophie a little more than two weeks earlier and the experience of that night still haunted me. As Frank I always seemed able to meet problems head on and now I found myself feeling a lot weaker when it came to having to deal with them. I was worried sick about having to tell her. It was difficult enough for an 18-year-old to have to deal with and now it was time to try and break the same shattering news to my baby girl who was just 12.

I woke up at 3.00 am, having only had about four hours sleep. Once again the dark thoughts had been around. I may have got over trying to take my own life, but that didn't stop me wanting to be dead. I actually began to pray God would take me in the night so that I could be at peace and join my dad. At least that way my secret would die with me and my family wouldn't have to cope with the public knowing about me and what I'd been hiding. I also kept getting a picture of Darren Sutherland in my head, remembering the way I'd found him. Hanging so still and looking so sad, but he was at peace. I wanted to be at peace and I truly believed death would bring the peace I wanted and solve the problems I was giving my family.

I was due to be at my old home for 7.00 pm. We'd had some great times in the house and I still had a lot of happy memories from years gone by, but now I hated going back. It was no longer part of me in the way it had been for so many years. Tracey had sent me a text asking if I wanted her and Sophie to have a word with Libby before I arrived. I was already on edge and the message just made me burst into tears. It made me realise yet again what I was doing to my baby girl. I was going to take away her dad and turn him into a woman. I got dressed in my Frank mode and drove over to pick up Emma before heading off to the house. Neither of us spoke very much and I could feel myself getting very tense and emotional. I'd been wrapping Christmas presents that afternoon and I couldn't stop crying as I did so. I knew that taking hormones was having an effect on my emotional state, but it wasn't just that. Libby was wise beyond her years and a strong little character, but nothing could possibly prepare her for the news I was going to give her.

Emma told me to stay strong. I knew she was right and that it was what I had to do, but I also knew how hard it was going to be. When we walked in both the girls were in their pyjamas. They were both smiling and seemed really happy. For an instant it felt as though I'd just dropped in for a quick visit, to have a cup of tea, laugh and joke the way we had in the past, but the thought was gone in a split second and the reality of exactly why I was there began to take over and drain my body. I felt physically weak and incredibly nervous. Tracey was there too and I could feel the emotion building within me. I wanted to turn around and run out of the house or have the ground open up and swallow me. Anything rather than face up to what I knew I must do. I wondered what sort of dad I really was. We swapped presents and drank tea, but then I knew I couldn't go on any longer.

'Libby,' I said. 'Come over here, little one, I've got to tell you dad's secret.'

I could feel the tears welling up in my eyes as I blinked to try and look around at everyone in the room. Sophie was looking anxiously at me. Tracey was looking at the floor. It must have been awful for both of them knowing what was about to be said. Once again I felt so guilty, thinking about the words I was about to deliver, words that could never be taken back. Emma told me once again to be strong. 'You can do it,' she insisted, knowing I was struggling.

Libby was next to me on the sofa and wriggling around, her head hanging over one of the cushions, her feet on my shoulder. I took hold of Libby's little head and held her tight. I wanted to hug her as closely as I could and tell her everything would be all right and how much I loved her.

'Well, are you going to tell me what's happening?' she asked. 'Are you ill, are you dying?'

I could hear the concern and hurt in her voice. I knew she had sensed I hadn't been myself in recent months and I think Libby felt there was something terrible going on. I tried to give her a little smile, but the tears were now rolling down my face. I started to tell her that I wasn't ill. I wanted to come right out with what was really going on, but I began to struggle to find the right words. At that moment Emma could see the look of puzzlement on Libby's face and she tried to reassure her.

'Libby,' she told her gently. 'Whatever dad tells you now, you have to remember he's always going to be your dad. He's told me this news and he's told Sophie, he also told your mum a long time ago.'

The tension in the room was unbearable and I knew I couldn't put the moment off any longer. Libby was getting more concerned. She could see this was serious but nobody was telling her anything. Then, finally, the words came spilling out, just as they had done when I'd told Tracey all those years ago, just as they had done when I told Emma and just as they had done when I'd told Sophie. 'I'm a transsexual,' I told her. 'I was born a boy, but I should have been like you, a little girl.'

I could see Libby was totally stunned and couldn't believe what had been said, what 12-year-old girl would? Emma came over and began stroking Libby's hair. I kept telling Libby how much I loved her and how sorry I was. I couldn't find the words I wanted to use. I was fumbling in the dark for them. I felt like I wanted to die there and then.

'Is this some sort of joke?' I could hear Libby asking. Then she repeated it, but there was no need for a reply, she could see that it wasn't. She looked at Tracey hoping her mum would tell her this whole thing wasn't happening.

'Libs, I wish it was a joke, but it's not,' I said, as I tried to regain control of my emotions. 'Do you want to talk to me about it?'

'No, I don't!' she said.

I could see the look of pain, hurt and confusion on her little face. I could also see that she was angry. The room we were sitting in was big but suddenly it began to feel very small. It seemed to be shrinking. It was as if there were too many people in a small space and there was nowhere for me to go, nowhere to hide, nowhere to run. I had exploded a bomb once more and all I could do was look at the damage. I knew Libby's life could never be the same again and it was all because of me. What had I just done to my baby girl? I almost ached with the pain of it all.

There was no point in me staying any longer. I knew it would just make matters worse. I had to leave. I somehow managed to mumble my goodbyes and Emma took my car keys, knowing I was in no fit state to drive. I knew what I had just done and I hated myself for it. We drove back in silence, neither of us really wanting to relive what had happened. I knew Libby had taken it badly and when I finally got back to my own house all I could do was sit in darkness and cry. I felt numb. I kept thinking about Libby's face and her asking me whether it was some sort of joke. The way she'd looked at me when I'd told her. It was one of the longest and loneliest nights of my life.

CHAPTER SEVENTEEN

Seeing in the new year

Seeing Libby so shocked and distressed to hear my secret was horrible. I knew she would need time to take it all in. It wasn't going to be easy for her. She had to try and come to terms with what was going to happen to her dad and there would be a lot of questions she needed answered. I was glad Sophie and Tracey would be with her.

I was sure a lot of things would start to fall into place for the girls now that they knew the truth and I was pleased that at last Tracey would not have to hide everything from them. At one stage I think Sophie had virtually accused Tracey of being responsible for what had gone wrong with our marriage. All the girls ever saw was the outside. The way I would often look tired and worn out. The way I'd suddenly snap. The way I'd become increasingly emotional and the way in which it looked as though there might be something seriously wrong with my health.

I went away for another TransLiving weekend not long after telling Libby and this time Emma came with me. She had seen pictures of Kellie but never actually met her. I knew she must be feeling uneasy, but when she turned up at my front door for the weekend she did a good job of hiding it and acted as though nothing was different. There was her dad dressed as a woman all ready and packed to go off for a transgender event. It must have seemed very weird but Emma was there for me, giving me the support she knew was so important. I also wanted her to meet some of the new friends I'd made and to get a glimpse of what life was like for so many transgender people.

When we got to our hotel in Bournemouth one of the first people we bumped into was Joy. She had been such a good friend to me and a tremendous help. I was glad that Emma was able to talk to her so soon after getting there. I'd brought four dresses with me and was desperate to make a favourable impression when Emma came to my room before we went down to dinner. I decided on wearing a black and red dress and when Emma arrived she smiled and said I looked good, but suggested that she help me tone down my make-up. I'd been dressing for some time, but I was playing catch-up in many ways and having my daughter there to offer help and advice was a new experience and one I really liked.

We had a nice meal and then Emma chatted to a few people, among them a genetic female who was there with her male partner dressed as a woman. I think it was a bit of an eye-opener but she liked the people she met, and that's the point really. They are people. We are people. Not freaks or perverts, just people. Some of those she met that weekend were transvestites, some were transsexuals who were not going to fully transition and some were people like me who had made the decision to fully transition.

The next day Emma met one girl who had invited her daughter and son-in-law to lunch with us. The daughter obviously knew all about her dad dressing and had been very supportive but it was the first time her husband had seen his father-in-law dressed as a woman. The party included three genetic women, one guy and the rest of us were dressed.

I think the weekend took its toll on Emma. It was bound to, but there was one really funny incident, when one of the girls paid Emma what she thought was a real compliment. 'That's one of the best hairpieces I've ever seen,' she said, looking at my daughter's real hair. I thought it was hilarious when she told me!

When Emma got back from Bournemouth she managed to tick another box for me when she told her children, Robyn and Ollie, about me. She made me laugh when she told me how she'd emphasised to Ollie that it was a secret and he mustn't tell anyone. 'I'm not exactly going to be talking to my mates about it, am I?' he joked. They were both lovely kids and I was lucky to have them as grandchildren. I was pleased that she'd told them and it must have made things easier for Emma and Richard. Having to keep such a big secret from your own kids is not nice, as I well knew.

After the weekend I felt as though there was a dark cloud hanging over me. I was due to travel to Spain in preparation for surgery. I wanted to say goodbye to Tracey and the girls before I went and I also wanted to see how Sophie and Libby were coping with all that had gone on. Sophie was watching television and Libby was upstairs in her room. I went into the kitchen with Tracey and as we drank tea, she began to cry. She was obviously very upset and I began to cry as well. I knew I'd ruined her life. We cuddled and I tried to tell her everything would be all right, but I think I was trying to convince myself as much as I was trying to reassure her. I said goodbye to Sophie and told her I'd see her after Christmas and then I went upstairs to see Libby. She seemed to be in her own little world and I wondered if she was still in shock. I sat in my car for quite a long time and once again the tears began to fall.

I was still in a dark mood the next day when I drove with my two dogs to catch the ferry. I stood on the deck with the wind blowing in my face and stared out to a sea that seemed to go on for ever. I thought briefly about what would happen if I jumped over the rail and into the water. The moment passed as quickly as it arrived, but I still didn't feel happy.

Emma was going to be flying out to meet me the following week while I was going to drive to my house in Portugal first and then go on to Spain and meet her at the airport. Emma could tell I was a bit down and tried to be very positive. She'd had quite a stressful few days herself. First there was seeing me dressed as Kellie for the first time, then she'd told her kids about me, and then she saw Jackie and told her mum that the man she had married had actually always been a woman. I'm sure Jackie was as shocked as you'd expect, but at least she now knew. I knew Emma loved me, but I also realised she loved her mum and saw her regularly. They got on really well and it must have been hard for Emma having to keep my secret back from her own mother.

The circle of people who now knew was growing. Apart from family members and Jan, there was also a close friend of mine and my lawyer, Neil Sibley. Emma had been to see Neil and explained everything to him. He was not only a good lawyer, he had also become a friend and I valued his advice and judgement. Neil was as good as gold when Emma told him and he advised me to close my Facebook and Twitter accounts and also my website. I wanted to disappear from public life completely and not have my privacy invaded.

Once I got to the house in Portugal I began to relax and feel much better about myself. The drive had done me good and helped to lift my mood. I was also looking forward to seeing Emma and having the surgery done. It meant a lot to me, not just because it was a feminisation process for my face, but because of what it meant. I was finally going to be taking the first surgical steps along the way to becoming a woman. I was going to have my trachea shaved, a lip lift, rhinoplasty and a jaw reshape. I felt excited by it all but at the same time a little nervous.

On the day I was due to meet Emma I set off at four in the morning to make sure I would be at Malaga airport with plenty of time to spare. I drove in Frank mode but suddenly panicked because I was going to be spending the next 12 days at the villa as Kellie and I didn't want the villa owner to see me as a man. I'd travelled to Spain with a hairpiece stuffed under my seat in the car and I also had a large pair of dark glasses in the glove compartment. I quickly stuffed the hairpiece on my head and put on the glasses only to see Emma laughing out loud. 'You look ridiculous, dad!' she said. 'You don't look like a woman you just look like a bloke in a wig and dark glasses.'

I looked in the mirror and had to agree she had a point and we both began to giggle at how silly I'd been. It was nice to be able to laugh at myself and I could see the funny side of things. I've never been someone who took themselves too seriously, and I didn't want that to change.

After a final consultation with the doctors at the hospital it was decided that I wouldn't have the jaw reshape and instead I would have a forehead lift. They said I had a lot of soft tissue around the jaw and the results would be better if I had the lift procedure. The whole idea was for me to make subtle changes to my face to feminise it and it was reassuring to know exactly what they were going to be doing to me. We met Anna, the hospital co-ordinator and Jenny, a transsexual girl, who worked with the facial feminisation team and provided support to the patients. I got on well with her and it was good having someone who I felt comfortable talking to.

The two of us were having lunch a day or two later while Emma went to collect Rich from the airport. It was the first time Rich had seen me as Kellie, but we just chatted in the way we always had done and there were no awkward moments. I realised it might have seemed a bit different for him – after all, it's not every day you sit down and have lunch with your father-in-law dressed as a woman, but he was very laid-back and understanding.

The procedure went well and although I had a lot of bruising, the doctors were pleased with the results. Having Emma and Rich there was a real help, but I knew they would have to go back to England and it was decided that Jenny would stay with me in the villa to offer support and help out with anything I needed. It was good to get that sort of aftercare and very reassuring to have her stay with me. When I went back to the hospital for my final check and to have some stitches removed they were really pleased with the results. I looked in the mirror and found myself feeling quite emotional. I wasn't sad, it was more a case of me actually beginning to look like the person I wanted to be.

Nine days after the operation I was allowed to travel back to my house in Portugal. It was four days before Christmas and I would be celebrating it on my own apart from my two lovely dogs. It was the way I had planned things and the way I wanted it. During my time in Spain I'd been in contact with Sophie and Libby, texting and talking. I knew it was still early days for them, but I'd already arranged for them to come out and visit me after Christmas and I was looking forward to them arriving.

I got to the house late and collapsed into bed, feeling relieved to be back in a place that felt like home, but the next day I had one of my emotional dips. I sat around crying and feeling depressed. It was as if I had no control over the way my mood would swing. I began to feel much better 24 hours later and decided to go shopping. I couldn't help thinking how different my life was from Christmas 12 months earlier. I didn't ever want to get into that terrible state again but I was aware that I was still fragile on occasions. I would worry about what was going to happen to me and what was going to happen to my family.

On Christmas Day I was up bright and early and sent a text to Libby because I knew she would be up early as well. She always was at Christmas. I sat drinking tea while I opened my cards from home and cried as I read them. It was a very emotional moment, but I wasn't going to let myself slip into a dark mood. Instead I opened my presents, got dressed in my Kellie mode and cooked Christmas lunch for me and the dogs. I was in constant contact via texts with all three girls. I knew they were having a good time and in my own way so was I. I didn't feel sad or upset, but contented. I thought of all the people who now knew about me, how I had shared my secret and how everyone had been so supportive.

I realised it was still very difficult for Sophie and Libby, but we were talking and joking. Time would help them and I knew I couldn't rush things. Emma had been amazing and I was aware that what was going on in my life had really taken over hers. She must have found it so difficult at times but she never complained. Tracey and I were now sorting out our divorce, we both still loved each other and I always wanted us to remain friends. As the light faded, I lit a big log fire, switched on the television and poured myself a couple of drinks. Christmas Day was coming to a close and I was in a happy place.

In the next few days I had some real dips in my mood. I experienced a lot of anxiety about exactly what Sophie and Libby thought of their dad. Lying in bed during the middle of the night, I would still have thoughts about death and whether it would be best for everyone if I was to just die peacefully. There were times when I would curl up and cry asking God to take me so that I could join my dad. They were very black moods and it was often difficult to shake them, but I wanted to see the New Year in by looking forward and by being the person I knew I wanted to be in 2014, by being Kellie.

On New Year's Eve I decided to go shopping at a mall in Faro. I remembered how different it had been for me five years earlier when I'd gone to Portugal after telling Tracey. How I'd desperately searched shops for female clothes and how badly dressed I was then compared to the way I now looked. When I thought about things like this I realised just how far I had come and how very simple and ordinary things were all part of the learning process for me and for other people who were transitioning.

I remembered once being in Boots back home in England, dressed as Kellie and buying a lot of make-up and cosmetics. When I went to pay for the sales assistant asked if I had a Boots card. I told her I did and then handed her one with the name of Frank Maloney on it! I bluffed my way out of it by saying it belonged to my boyfriend. I also learned from a girl at one of Linda's social evenings how to get a credit card in a female name. Just phone up and say you want one for your girlfriend. I ended up with three different cards, making it so much easier to shop.

I decided to head along the coastline and go for a meal at a place called Quarteira. I parked the car and began to walk towards the seafront where I knew there were quite a few restaurants. By this time it was dark and I found myself walking down a dimly lit alley. I'd walked down similar roads before and not thought anything of it, but I heard footsteps behind me and suddenly felt very vulnerable. It was an odd feeling. I'd walked through some of the worst areas of London and New York as Frank and not been bothered at all, but here I was as Kellie walking down a narrow street in Portugal and feeling really anxious about who might be behind me. I'd enjoyed a really nice afternoon shopping and had noticed how much nicer people seemed to treat you when you were a woman, but I realised there was another side to being out on your own as a female.

I reached the seafront and felt relieved to see the restaurants. I ordered a meal and some wine and then sat there on my own and looked around. Most of the other tables were occupied by couples out for a meal together. I began to wonder if it was always going to be like this for me now, a table for one on New Year's Eve. I began to feel a bit sad and realised that perhaps going out on my own was not the best of ideas. I ate my meal and left. It was still relatively early and Frank would probably have looked for a bar to go into for a couple drinks, but there was no way I was going to do that as Kellie. I just wanted to get home, but as I drove my mood began to get darker.

By the time I reached the house I was in a real state. I sat in the car crying and began praying to God for strength asking why I felt the way I did, and I started talking out loud to my dad, asking him for his help. I looked in the rear view mirror at myself and saw my eye make-up streaming down my face. I looked awful and I knew I had to pull myself together. I went into the house and began binging on biscuits and cake before dragging myself off to bed at about 10.45 pm. I took a couple of pills to help me sleep and eventually drifted off, thinking about the fact that this was probably the first ever time in my adult life I'd been in bed before midnight on a New Year's Eve. My life really was changing.

CHAPTER EIGHTEEN

Under siege

I began 2014 in a positive frame of mind because I knew that Sophie and Libby were arriving to spend a few days with me in Portugal. It gave me a real lift to see their faces when they came through arrivals. I was dressed in my Frank mode and it was lovely to be able to cuddle them once again. I was prepared to answer any questions they might have, but at the same time realised that it probably wasn't a good idea for me to push things. They had to get used to this in their own time and at their own pace. I was just happy to have them with me, and the time seemed to fly by while they were there, but seeing them off at the airport was tough. Yet again I found myself in tears and Sophie asked why I was crying. The combination of the sadness I felt at them going coupled with the effect of the hormones I was taking made me feel very emotional.

I stayed in Portugal for another couple of weeks before travelling back to England. I'd had my bad moments while I was out there but, but overall the trip had gone well, and I felt quite sad at having to leave. I knew the coming year was going to bring about a lot of change in my life. Things would be different for me, but as I walked the dogs on my birthday on board the ferry that was taking us back to England I at least had the feeling I was more in control of my life. I had a lovely time the day I got back. We had a family meal and celebrated my birthday. It made me feel really happy and at the same time very grateful that everyone had given me such great support.

I gradually began to get back into the swing of things after being away for nearly two months. I started my electrolysis treatment once more and also had to pay a visit to the gender clinic in London. Everything went well and there were no problems. I'd managed to meet Emma and Rich for a coffee before the appointment and it felt good to be walking around town in my Kellie mode. I was doing this more and more, although there were still occasions when I would have to be dressed as Frank.

I was happy and contented as I got on the train that day with my coffee and a copy of the *Evening Standard*, but then I heard a voice behind me that sent a shiver down my spine. A man was talking on his mobile phone and then sat directly opposite me. I recognised him immediately. I should have done, because I'd known him for about 30 years. His name was Harry Cowap, and he was a former boxer. A really nice guy and in other circumstances I would have started chatting to him but I was petrified. He stared right at me, but didn't have a clue as to who I was and in many ways I suppose it was a compliment. He just saw me as a woman and that was all I ever wanted to be anyway, but my nerves were jangling the entire time he was on the train. I breathed a sigh of relief when he got off.

Just over a week later the feeling of being in control that I'd had on the ferry and the relief I'd felt at hiding my true identity on the train were shattered. At about 4.30 pm on a Thursday afternoon there was a knock at my front door. When I opened it I was confronted by someone who told me they were from the *Sun*. They had got pictures of me dressed as Kellie and wanted to talk to me about whether I'd been dressing as a woman. The blood must have drained from my face, but I immediately denied it was me and said that the whole thing was a load of rubbish. I shut the door and could feel my heart pounding. I had known this day might come, but I hadn't been prepared for it. In an instant it felt as though my world was caving in. The story was out there and a national newspaper had it. They might not be able to confirm it right now, but I knew how newspapers worked. It wasn't a case of if I would be exposed it was more a case of when.

When I saw the pictures I knew where they had been taken and I had my suspicions about who might have set me up, but in many ways that didn't really matter. The fact was I had to try and find a way to stop this story coming out. I spoke to Tracey and Emma on the phone and they could both tell I was in shock. My lawyer Neil went into action, but before seeing him I drove to Tracey's and asked my mum to come over so that we could talk about what it meant for the family.

All I could see in my head were lurid headlines and my picture splashed all over the front page. It wasn't just about me, but it was also about my family and the effect this could have on them. I suddenly began to feel weak and worried. When we met at Tracey's I found out that her sister Kim and her brother Rob had been contacted by reporters as well. It was going from bad to worse and I broke down. This was all my fault and I said out loud that I wished I was dead. My mum put her arms around me and told me that I had to be strong and that the most important people in my life were behind me.

'Don't worry about anyone else,' she told me. 'How do you think I would feel if I had to bury you before me? We all need you to be strong; together we can beat this. If this story does come out, it will be like you've always said. In two weeks' time it'll just be chip paper.'

I had my meeting with Neil and a QC which went well. They would try everything they could do to keep the story appearing in the press, but we all knew that it would at some stage come out. I just wanted to have some degree of control over it. Neil called the next night while we were having a family meal at a Chinese restaurant and I saw Emma smile with relief. I began to cry. Tracey put her arms around me and told me not to let Libby see me with tears again. In the days that followed I fully expected something to appear, but it didn't happen. We had bought ourselves some time, but the threat was hanging over me and over all the family.

I had already made contact with a celebrity management agency called Champions UK. After the brush with the *Sun* I met with their CEO, John Hayes, and his son, Matt, who was the managing director of the company. I went in my Frank mode with Emma and had a really good meeting. I liked John and although I couldn't tell him exactly what was going on, I did hint at there being a big problem in my life of a very personal nature. We agreed that we would meet again in a month's time to talk further and then go to a dinner they were having in Nottingham.

At that next meeting I asked them to sign a non-disclosure agreement and then told them exactly what was going on in my life, including the fact that the press had got wind of the whole thing. It was good to get things out in the open and although I could see that John was stunned, his reaction was very good and he tried to reassure me. I knew that if I was going to face any media storm that might be brewing I couldn't really do it on my own and their organisation seemed well-equipped and experienced in crisis management.

We decided to put out a simple press statement to take the sting out of any story and to coincide with the half-term holiday at the end of May. The last thing I wanted was Libby or Ollie to have to go into school after the story was plastered all over the newspapers. After a family meeting, late afternoon on 23 May was earmarked as the time and date of the release. My mother went off to visit family and friends in Ireland and was due to return on the date of the press release, but then we decided against the strategy. Mum, who hadn't realised about the change in plan, told my brother Eugene. As expected, his reaction wasn't good but at least he now knew.

It began to feel as though there was a ticking bomb waiting to explode, but the longer things went on without any story appearing in the papers the more I believed that perhaps I would get the time and space I wanted to sort myself out before anything became public knowledge. I carried on with preparations for transition which included having voice coaching and at the end of May I underwent a procedure to give me a more feminine hairline. I had 1,850 hairs from the back of my head transplanted to the front. It was all part of what I knew I had to do if I was going to feel comfortable in my new life and look the way I wanted to. I was booked in for yet another electrolysis session on the first Saturday in June, but the evening before I got a shocking call from Emma. A reporter had paid a visit to her house. Robyn had answered the door and thought the reporter worked for the *Sunday Sun*. Rich then joined Robyn and refused to speak to the reporter who had wanted to talk to Emma about me. We put in a call to Neil and he seemed puzzled by the whole thing because he believed the threat from the *Sun* had been dealt with.

While I was having the painful electrolysis treatment the next day, a woman called from the *Sunday People* to say they had pictures of me living as a woman and they were going to run them the next day. Robyn must have misheard the reporter the previous evening when they said where they were from. My whole body went into shock and I began trembling, but I knew I couldn't allow my nerves to get the better of me while I was talking to her. I denied everything and then said that if they were going to try and publish anything they'd be hearing from my lawyer.

I was newsworthy enough for the tabloid press. The transgender and boxing worlds were not usually mentioned in the same sentence and the fact that I'd managed the heavyweight champion of the world made it even more of a story. I immediately phoned Emma and Neil to let them know what had happened. My phone rang again and as soon as I saw the name 'Ian' on the display I not only knew who it was but also what the call was going to be about.

I'd known Ian for some years and liked him. He was married to the sister of Caroline, the girl I'd had a relationship with before meeting Tracey. He'd been a news editor and assistant editor in News International and he'd also once worked for the *People* but he now had his own multimedia public relations company.

'I know what this is about,' I told him. We arranged to meet in a hotel just off the A3 in Cobham, Surrey. I knew that Ian was aware of the *People* story and that's why he phoned. He explained that the picture desk had sent him the pictures they were proposing to use because they were aware that he knew me. I didn't see the point in trying to lie to Ian and so I was straight with him and said that I'd had a problem all my life and that I was transsexual. We were sitting in the lobby of the hotel and it was quite crowded. I was in a real state and could feel myself shaking. I sat there with a pair of large dark glasses covering my eyes and did my best to conceal the fact that I was crying behind them.

He showed me the pictures and apart from the ones that the *Sun* reporter had shown me, there were a couple of others, neither of which were particularly flattering. I knew immediately when they'd been taken because it was the day after I'd had my hair procedure and I was walking my dogs near the house in Maidstone. I'd just thrown on some old clothes. I'm not sure what was more shocking. The way I looked in them or the fact that there had obviously been a photographer lurking outside and I hadn't realised it.

Ian insisted he could help and I was aware that he knew his way around the tabloid press and he still had very good contacts. Between him and Neil I hoped that they would be able to stop publication. Neil had been in a meeting that morning and so I had left a message. He rang back to say that he was going to make contact with the paper and try to get the story stopped even though I knew by now that they were planning to splash it all across their front page. Ian had to leave and I waited anxiously to hear from Neil and made calls to Tracey and Emma. Both of them could tell I was in a real state. I kept wondering what would happen if the story broke the next day. How would little Libby cope at school? Sophie was due to start a new job – how would she feel facing her new colleagues? The tension was unbearable and I could physically feel the pressure on my body. It was as if I was being squeezed and the life sucked out of me. I'd never felt so helpless in my life. All I could do was wait and hope.

At exactly 3.35 pm my phone rang once more and I could see it was Neil. I answered it instantly and he gave me the news.

The *People* were going to pull the story. The relief was unbelievable. Another attempt to expose my private life had been stopped, but I knew I might not be so fortunate next time and if there was one thing I was absolutely certain of, it was that there would be a next time.

CHAPTER NINETEEN

Facing the press

I couldn't go on hoping the story of my gender transition would not come out. It was only a matter of time before something was printed and the best scenario for me was to make sure that I had a degree of control.

Four days after my scare at the weekend Emma and I went for a meeting with Neil and Ian in London. We had a long discussion about what had already happened and what might happen. It might be best to give the story exclusively to a newspaper that would handle it sympathetically and allow us some degree of control. We went through various options and Ian suggested we try the *Sunday Mirror*. He was to make the initial contact and we would see if something could be worked out. I came away from the meeting feeling better about things.

The negotiations seemed to go on forever. In fact, it took about four or five weeks, during which time I was on an emotional rollercoaster. So too was Emma and the rest of the family. It finally looked as though everything had been agreed and that the story would be coming out at the end of July. I would do the interview in the week leading up to publication date, but just when we got that far there was yet another issue with the contract and the whole thing was put back. I felt terrible. I'd already geared myself up to do the interview on 23 July and when it was postponed I had a sick feeling in my stomach. My emotions were once again all over the place and I just wanted this thing done and out of the way. I was angry and frustrated until, much to my relief we settled on an interview on 31 July with the story to be published on either Sunday 3 August or a week later on 10 August. At least I was now able to prepare myself properly for what was to come. There was no turning back. I had to get ready to tell the world about being a transsexual.

The interview was going to take place at a hotel near Maidstone and when I drove over to pick up Emma I could hardly stop my knees from trembling. I was incredibly nervous and almost felt like pulling out, but I knew I couldn't do that. I'd arranged to have Heather Ashton from my support group, TG Pals, come along to the interview. The group had been so important and Heather had been there to offer help, advice and guidance throughout, just as she had for everyone who attended the meetings.

As a transgender person you often feel very alone in the world, with nobody to talk to or understand what you're going through. Going to TG Pals helped me to realise that no matter how bad things seemed at times, there were people out there who were ready to help.

What lots of people don't realise is just how much you lose when you are transgender. You can often lose your partner, family, job, friends, in fact all the things that have been so important in your life. If there had been a support group like TG Pals around when I was younger who knows what might have happened? I had been desperate for knowledge and some sort of support. The world has changed and thanks to people like Heather and her group people are now being helped in the way they need. Having her along at the interview was important and so too was having Emma.

I walked through the entrance of the hotel with Emma and Heather, feeling terrible. I was wearing a long blue dress and hid my eyes behind a large pair of dark glasses. They covered quite a bit of my face and I felt as though I was hiding behind them.

Matthew Drake, the reporter who was going to do the interview, jumped up from his seat as we walked in. He led us to a room at the hotel and tried to make us all feel comfortable. The room was dark and quite stuffy. It was a hot day and there didn't seem to be much air. I got the impression that he wasn't really expecting me to have people with me and he was also surprised when a digital recorder was produced so that I could keep a record of what was going to be said. For the first ten or 15 minutes I was very defensive and, on occasion, aggressive as he began to ask questions, but then the tension eased a little and I began to relax.

I found myself shedding some tears as I recounted parts of my life which until then had remained private. It was an emotional experience and to be fair to Matthew he handled what was often a difficult and awkward situation well. I found the whole thing incredibly draining, but once it was over I had a feeling of relief and I felt the worst was over. It had been decided that the story would be published on 10 August, so all we could do was wait.

Emma came over to my house to help me choose the right outfits for the photoshoot the following day. It was going to take place in a different hotel and I knew I was also going to be answering a few extra questions. I took quite a long time getting ready and deciding on what to wear. I smiled as I was doing this because it was in marked contrast to what I would have been like preparing for something like this as Frank. I'd have grabbed the first pair of jeans I could find, taken a shirt out of the wardrobe and stuck on a pair of shoes as I went out of the front door.

The shoot turned out to be very enjoyable. I got on really well with the photographer and the make-up artist was really good as well. The whole atmosphere was very different to the way it had been the day before, and I was much more relaxed with Matthew. Emma and I left, knowing that the next nine days weren't going to be easy. Apart from waiting to see what Matthew was going to do with the story and what the pictures would look like, there was also another important job to be done before the story was published and I wasn't really looking forward to it.

There was a group of six people that Emma and I thought should be told before the story actually broke. They were all friends and it was decided that she would go to see two of them and tell them face-to-face, phone two others and I would phone the other two. There was also another friend who we were going to tell, but he'd managed to guess a few weeks earlier. He'd seen the way I'd changed and the way I'd been acting and pretty much came to the conclusion that I was becoming more feminine every time we met. When Emma confirmed everything to him I know it was a shock and the whole thing messed his head up, but he didn't say that he didn't want to see me again. I knew that he needed his own time to come to terms with what had happened.

The two friends Emma phoned couldn't get their heads around what she was telling them and, sadly, I haven't had any real contact with them since. The other two that she went to see were Tommy Pratt and Ray Hawkins. Both of them had been great friends to me and I was worried about how they might take the news. I didn't want to lose their friendship, but I was prepared for that and I wasn't going to blame them. Emma stayed with them for about two hours explaining as much as she could and they were both great about it, even though they must have been struggling to take it all in. Ray kept saying, 'I don't believe it,' over and over again, but they were both brilliant about the whole thing. They told Emma I was still their friend and when she let me know I felt like a weight had been lifted from me. It was so good to know that I still had their friendship and I realised that hearing the news couldn't have been easy for them, but I subsequently received a text from Tommy that was fantastic and a real boost.

'Hey Frank,' he wrote. 'I want to tell you it doesn't matter to me. We will always love you for what you are inside.'

I was going to phone Guy Williamson and Joe Dunbar. Although I'd known Guy for many years I called his wife Hazel. I was very nervous. 'Hazel,' I said. 'Guy's been my friend for years and I've got something very personal to tell him, but I don't feel I can tell him face to face. This thing is going to come out in the papers on Sunday.'

'That's okay,' she told me. 'You haven't murdered anyone have you?' she asked and I smiled because Guy is now a successful barrister.

'No, nothing like that,' I laughed and then came straight to the point. 'Hazel, all my life I've lived with a personal problem. I'm a transsexual.'

'Oh, that's all right,' she said reassuringly and then listened as I told her that I was quite a long way down the transition route. She was great about the whole thing and then joked with me that if Guy didn't like it when she told him, he could pack his bags and go! Guy called me that same night and we talked for ages.

'You've been my friend for years and yet you tell Hazel before you tell me,' he said and then asked if he could still call me Frank.

'Guy, you can call me Frank. In fact, you can call me whatever you want, as long as we maintain our friendship,' I told him.

It was so good to hear him being so understanding and I was equally pleased with the reaction I got from Joe. I'm sure he was surprised but you would never have known it from his reaction on the phone and we just chatted in the way we normally would have done. At the end of the conversation he said that he was so glad I'd told him and I knew he meant it. I was lucky to have friends like Guy, Tommy, Ray and him.

It was Thursday evening. I was due to travel down to Ilfracombe with my friend Roz the next day and the story would be out on Sunday. The clock was ticking.

CHAPTER TWENTY

A sense of relief

I had told my story to the *Mirror* and now I could only wait. I settled into our chalet at the holiday complex in Devon and I began
to feel happier and more relaxed. I knew what was going to be
written, because as part of the agreement with the *Mirror* we
were allowed to see the copy a few days earlier. There had been
one or two minor things that we asked to be changed, more to
do with terminology, but overall I thought they had done exactly
what they said they were going to do. It was very professional
and also very sympathetic.

I also got to see what the pages would look like and I was
pleased with all of the photographs they'd taken. I felt relaxed,
but I still thought it was better if I took a couple of sleeping pills
before I went to bed. I wanted to get a good night's sleep and be
prepared for whatever was in store for me the next day. There was
no stopping what was going to happen so there was also no point
in worrying too much about it. I'd done enough of that already. I

had planned and prepared for the moment this time. Of course I was nervous, who wouldn't be?

But at the same time this was not like it had been when I almost had a meltdown at the hotel in Cobham when I thought the *People* might be running a story on me the next day or the way I felt the blood drain from me when I was confronted by the *Sun* journalist. It had been almost exactly six months since that day and I'd had to live with the threat of exposure throughout that period while still trying to carry on leading my life. It had made me nervy and cautious and my family had to deal with me being like that.

There were times when I'd been paranoid, like the occasion I was convinced there was a reporter lurking outside my house. I'd even phoned Emma. It turned out to be nothing more than a local taxi driver having a sleep after a nightshift. That's how crazy it had become and that's why I wanted to end the wait for what was becoming more inevitable by the day.

I had concerns about being recognised by people in the complex where we were staying. I'd used a dark hairpiece for the photoshoot and I'd brought a blonde one with me to Devon. I also had my big, dark glasses and a pair of clear-glass glasses which made me look a bit different.

I wanted to see the papers and Roz went to get them. We both looked through them and it was obvious the *Sunday Mirror* had got the exclusive they wanted and we both agreed that they'd done a very good job. The story was fair and balanced, and they'd even included a piece from Heather about transsexualism as well as the contact details for TG Pals, which was just the sort of thing I wanted to get greater publicity for.

The story was about me in one way, but in another sense it wasn't. I had a voice that was being heard and a platform to try and get across to the public just what it was like for a transsexual. People might be reading about Kellie Maloney but my thoughts, emotions, problems and the inner battle I waged with myself for my entire life will have struck a familiar chord with other transsexuals. The heartache of being true to yourself and true to your feelings is enormous. I have girlfriends who are never allowed to dress in front of their children. I even knew one who had been completely cut off by her children who refused to accept that their father was really a woman. They wouldn't even go and see her when she was dying in a hospital bed. Ask yourself how awful that must have been. I'm not saying everything is doom and gloom, but what I will say is that it is never easy for transsexuals, simply because they have to make such life-changing decisions which not only affect them but their closest family and friends.

The Champions agency had arranged to have someone take care of all my phone calls and text messages. I had the use of another mobile which only a chosen few people had. Even then they had to contact me and then I would get back to them.

When the wider media got wind of the story everything went wild. I had prepared myself for the worst, but couldn't have been more surprised by what began to happen throughout the day. Far from being ridiculed as I had once thought might happen, I immediately started getting messages of support on social media. The television and radio stations were also very positive and people reviewing the papers were kind and generous about me and the way they thought I'd been brave to come out and tell my story in a very public manner.

Poor Emma was upset that she wasn't around while this was happening. She'd already booked a holiday with Rich and Ollie in Portugal, but it didn't take her long to make contact on my new mobile and I think we both felt relieved at what was now happening and how the news had been received. My big fear about the boxing world proved to be unfounded, and lots of people went on social media to offer their support including Lennox Lewis. 'I was as shocked as anyone at the news about my former promotor and my initial thought was it was a wind-up,' said Lewis. 'The great thing about life and boxing, is that you never know what to expect. This world isn't always cut and dried or black-and-white and coming from the boxing fraternity, I can only imagine what a difficult decision this must be for Kellie.'

'However, having taken some time to read Kellie's statements, I understand better what she, and others in similar situations, are going through. I think that *all* people should be allowed to live in a way that brings them harmony and inner peace. I respect Kellie's decision and say if this is what brings about true happiness in her life, then so be it.'

It was nice to see the statement from him and from others, some of them famous, lots of them just ordinary men and women who offered their support. It was very touching to read, and the next day my story continued to be big news in all the newspapers and broadcast media. There were phone-ins devoted to transgender issues and other transsexuals were invited on radio and television shows to talk about their experiences and give their views. It was crazy but at the same time very positive and I hoped that my story had at least opened the door for others, allowing the public to begin understanding a world very few of them knew anything about.

Champions had been inundated with requests for interviews with me and by the time Tuesday arrived it was clear things were not going to calm down. Someone said to me that the story had managed to change the news agenda in the UK. I wasn't sure whether that was true, but I was sure there was now no need for me to be in Ilfracombe. I had booked the place for a week thinking I might need to keep a low profile and hide away for a few days. I certainly could not have expected things to have gone as well as they did.

It was time for me to join the real world once more, although in the few days which were to follow, I began to realise just how unreal my world had suddenly become.

CHAPTER TWENTY-ONE

Big Brother

The reaction to my story being published was overwhelming. It was better than anything I could have hoped for or imagined. There had been a few silly comments made on social media but they were the exception and overall the public had been fantastic. To have that sort of genuine support made things so much easier for me and my family. For months and weeks I'd been worried about my secret becoming public, and about the effect it would have on my family. None of us really knew what the fallout would be. The one thing I am sure about is that none of us believed it would be as positive as it turned out to be.

I drove back to London two days after the story had appeared in the *Sunday Mirror* and stayed in a hotel not too far from the ITV television studios because the next day I had agreed to do an interview for *Good Morning Britain*. It was just one of a number of offers my management company had received since my story became public and they had been busily sifting through everything. I was going to meet Champions' Matthew and his as-sistant Amelia Neate to discuss various proposals and then spend the day with them after the interview having some meetings.

Emma was still in Portugal, but Sophie had agreed to come with me and this was the first time she had seen Kellie in the flesh. She was really good and also gave me advice on my make-up and the type of clothes I should wear for the interview. She was as relieved as I was at the public's response, but I think we were also both a bit bewildered by the continuing media interest and how the whole transgender issue had been given so much exposure. As far as I was concerned it could only be a good thing if it got people talking about the subject and wanting to under-stand it more.

The interview on *Good Morning Britain* went really well. I had felt quite relaxed about it because I knew that Ben Shepherd was one of the presenters, and I'd known him since he'd taken part in the celebrity boxing I became involved with some years ear-lier. But when I got to the studios I found out it was his day off. Susanna Reid and John Stapleton did the interview, and I felt incredibly nervous as I sat opposite them. I'd sat in dozens of studios over the years and answered all sorts of questions but that was as Frank Maloney. This was the first time Kellie was going to be seen on national television and it all felt very different. I was much more aware of the way I looked, acted and sounded, but the two of them were excellent and really made me feel at ease. I slowly began to enjoy the experience thanks to the way they handled it, and came away from the studios in a happy frame of mind and ready for a meeting that I knew could have conse-quences for me on all sorts of levels.

I can't say that I'd ever been an avid watcher of *Big Brother*. I knew it was very popular and both Sophie and Libby would watch it when it was on, but I didn't really know much about it other than the fact that a group of people who had never met before were thrown together in a house for weeks on end. The celebrity version of the show was also very popular and the latest series of it was due to begin in less than a week. They had made contact with Matthew and asked if I would be interested in taking part.

I'd spent a year trying to avoid publicity. When I made the decision to tell my story I did so because I hated the idea of being exposed and because I knew that sooner or later the news of my private life would leak out. Once I'd retired from boxing and took myself out of public life, all I wanted to do was melt into the background and keep as low a profile as possible. I wasn't sure I was ready to deal with what might happen on *Big Brother*. I had serious doubts about whether I would be able to cope with living 24 hours a day with a bunch of strangers while at the same time having pretty much everything I did filmed for the benefit of the viewing public. It was a risk and a gamble, I knew that. I was in a very vulnerable place in my life. I was still very emotional and I'd lived a pretty solitary life for quite a long time. Stepping into the *Big Brother* house could be disastrous.

We met with the producers of the programme and talked everything through. In principle I began to think that perhaps it wouldn't be such a bad idea. It was a chance for me to have a voice and talk about transgender issues openly on national television. It might be a chance for the public to see and get to understand what it is like to be a transsexual. I knew it wasn't just about me beating the drum for the transgender community. There was also a commercial aspect involved because I hadn't really earned any money for more than a year. The more I thought about it the more I believed it might be a good idea, but I also knew instinctively there would be at least one person in my family who might not agree.

Emma was still on holiday in Portugal but we had kept in contact each day and she knew what had been going on with me and the great reaction I'd got from the public. She had been there for me whenever I'd need her and never stopped giving me support. I knew that she would not want me to do *Big Brother* and I was right. I realised she was worried about me going into the house and being watched 24 hours a day, seven days a week. She was very protective of me and the last thing I wanted was to upset her but I began to feel that the positives of taking part outweighed the negative aspects.

My life had undergone such a massive change in the space of just a few days and the reaction to the story remained good. News of what was happening with me had even spread to the continent and I was invited to attend a boxing promotion in Germany. The show was being staged by the Sauerland organisation, and I'd had quite a bit to do with them over the years. I was also asked to do a newspaper interview for *Bild*. I couldn't really believe the interest and everything seemed to be happening so quickly. I didn't have time to think but I'd be lying if I said I wasn't enjoying it. The relief I'd felt on the morning after the story was published continued throughout the week and all the fears I'd had for so long began to melt away.

I'd hidden myself away for so long and agonised about what life would be like for me as Kellie. Now I was beginning to find out, but it was nothing like anything I could have imagined. I almost had to pinch myself at times to make sure it was all actually happening. I'd had enough nightmare moments over the years and now it felt like I was living a very different dream.

I flew to Germany with Linda on the Friday of that week and we were due to spend two days there. By this time I had pretty much agreed to do *Celebrity Big Brother*. I was nervous about it, but thought that it would also help me in many other ways as Kellie. I was well aware that this was still very early days for me and also that I was very emotional. I still had the odd occasion when I felt anxious and sad. As well as the world getting to know Kellie, Kellie was getting to know the real world.

I believed I was strong enough to cope with going into the house. I'd been a strong character all of my life and Kellie was no different to Frank. As Frank Maloney I think I always possessed the ability to find humour in all sorts of situations and also to laugh at myself. I've never thought you should take yourself too seriously and I had no intention of changing my thinking once I started living life full-time as Kellie. I'd also decided that the money I would earn from the programme would not only help me but my family and I wanted to be able to donate a decent amount to Heather and her TG Pals organisation. They helped me through some pretty bleak moments in my life and I wanted to help make sure they were able to do the same for others.

I travelled to Germany dressed casually and armed with a letter from my transgender clinic. I needed this because I was still using my Frank Maloney passport and turning up as Kellie with a picture of Frank could cause confusion. The letter confirmed that I was in the process of undergoing gender reassignment. I passed through security but as I walked through a scanner it began to bleep. I was asked to go through again and the same thing happened. A female security official gave me a quick patdown and then asked me to go through the scanner once more and I set the machine off again.

'I'm afraid we're going to have to ask you to go into a little room over there for a more thorough body search, madam,' she told me. At this point I couldn't help breaking into giggles which probably didn't go down too well with the security people. I couldn't help thinking to myself, boy, is she in for a surprise! In the room I explained that I was a transsexual and asked whether it was going to cause any problems. She was perfectly fine about it and we discovered it had been my girdle which had set off the machines. She told me it might be a good idea for me not to travel through security with it in the future.

I remembered a couple of other recent moments that I'd found equally amusing. There was the occasion when I'd been dressed as Frank and went to a coffee shop. I'd been to the same place a few weeks earlier in my Kellie mode and had to use the toilet so when I went back as Frank, I knew exactly where they were. I marched straight into the ladies, forgetting how I was dressed and who I was supposed to be. I quickly had to apologise to the owner and said I hadn't been looking where I was going. I think I also managed to confuse one of my neighbours when I was walking my dogs dressed as Kellie, having previously taken them out dressed as Frank.

'Oh,' she said. 'I usually see your husband walking the dogs.'

'I've given him the day off today,' I told her.

In Germany I did the newspaper interview the day I arrived and they took me to the Brandenburg Gate to have my picture taken. The story appeared in the sports section the next day. I was also given a really nice reception at the boxing promotion on the Saturday night. I had been incredibly nervous about the reception I might get. I sent a text to Emma as I missed her very much and I was feeling quite down. I'd experienced a lot of euphoria since the story on Sunday and I suppose I was always going to hit a bit of a wall emotionally.

I'd made the decision to go into the *Big Brother* house and Matthew and Neil had been working on making sure all the conditions I needed were in place. I knew it was a risk, but I didn't want to back out now. I also knew that Emma was upset with me for agreeing to do the show and was worried about the effect it could have on me. This began to play on my mind but I hoped that ultimately she would understand why I had agreed.

When I picked up my ticket at the arena that evening I was shaking with nerves, but I tried to pull myself together and walked to my ringside seat. I recognised several boxing people and at first thought they might be trying to avoid me, but nothing could have been further from the truth. Not only did they acknowledge me, they also went out of their way to come and speak to me. They couldn't have been nicer, and before too long all my nerves had disappeared. It had been more than a year since I'd been to a boxing promotion and I have to say it made me realise that the sport was still in my blood.

One of the nicest things to happen that night was meeting a guy called Luan Krasniqi. He was a former European heavyweight champion who I had promoted in the late 1990s and who had been based in Germany before retiring. He admitted he'd been shocked when he read about me but then said how brave I was to be doing what I was doing. I'd also bumped into another ex-fighter earlier at my hotel and had a similar response. I had been waiting to check in when I suddenly felt a tap on my shoulder and turned to see the familiar face of American Joey Gamache, a two-time world champion. He was now training one of the boxers on the promotion. 'Kellie, one of the greatest promoters in boxing,' he said smiling at me. 'Just wanted to come and say, "Hello" and also say I've got real respect for what you're doing.' It was a really nice thing to hear and I could tell that he genuinely meant it. He could quite easily have avoided me if he'd wanted to.

All the people I met on the night were equally supportive. It was a really enjoyable experience and also a boost to my confidence. It made me think how nice most people were but the next morning an airport official proved to be the exception to the rule. I spotted him just as we were about to get our passports checked.

'Watch this,' I told Linda. 'I bet I get stopped.'

Sure enough, I was right. This guy had a shaven head and a real scowl on his face. I gave him my passport and the letter from the clinic. He looked at me with complete contempt in his eyes. 'This is not you,' he said, looking at me and then looking at the passport picture and as he did so I could see his contempt growing.

'Yes, it is,' I insisted. 'Here's a letter from my doctor to explain why I don't look like that anymore, I'm in the process of changing my sex. I'm a transsexual.'

I actually felt good about confronting this guy. I knew he understood exactly what was going on with me but I got the feeling that he didn't have a particularly high opinion of transgender people. He was determined to make things as difficult and awkward as he could. I stared him straight in the eye to see what his next move might be. Would he dispute what I was telling him or call his boss? Instead, he just chucked the passport back at me and flicked his head to motion me through. Everyone I had met in Germany could not have been nicer and then right at the end of the trip I had to come into contact with someone like him. It was a shame, but I enjoyed standing up for myself.

The flight back to London was peaceful enough but my arrival was not. Nothing had yet been signed off for *Big Brother* yet newspapers were claiming that I was going to be getting £400,000 for taking part, which was way off the mark. I was feeling pretty tired and emotional about everything as I made my way to arrivals at Heathrow I phoned Amelia at Champions and told her that they needed to ask for more money. I couldn't help myself. I think it was the Frank in me that prompted it. I'd read the story quoting a much bigger figure than I was getting, so if nothing had been signed and sealed then why didn't we ask for more? Poor Amelia must have wondered what had hit her. I was suddenly nothing like the polite, smiling Kellie she had been with just a few days earlier. She was getting a taste of the old Frank.

The thought of going into the house was beginning to get to me. I'd spent the weekend going through the plusses and minuses of taking part. I'd decided to go ahead with it but I suddenly began to feel the pressure of that decision and I think it got to me a bit. To top it all, the car which was supposed to pick me up hadn't arrived and I was beginning to throw a bit of a tantrum. I was standing next to a guy who was there for a pick up and he was holding up a piece of paper with his client's name on it. He was a big guy and glanced down as he saw me trying to make a call. I think he may have recognised me from all the publicity I'd been getting that week and he gave me a nod and a smile. In normal circumstances I would have smiled back and acknowledged him, but by this time I was getting so wound up that all this man heard was me shouting.

'Amelia,' I suddenly said. 'If the car's not here in five minutes they can stick their *Big Brother* up their arses!' Hardly the most ladylike thing to shout out in the middle of an arrivals hall and my only excuse was that I was strung out. I'd had a week of highs and now I felt myself spiralling towards a big low.

The fee was eventually negotiated and Libby and Sophie came to help me pack, along with Heather. We all discussed how I should act in the house. And then it was time to be taken by car to the hotel. I was in a bad way and began to wonder why I had agreed to do the show. Perhaps it had all come too quickly for me and I should have said 'no'? I began to panic about what I'd landed myself with, but right on cue some champagne arrived and I quickly drank a couple of glasses. I felt slightly better as the alcohol began to take effect and then went ahead with a photo-shoot for the show. I began to realise just what a big operation the whole thing was and saw the degree of secrecy that was involved.

The television in the hotel was switched off and I was no longer Kellie but had instead been given the code name of KitKat. It was real cloak-and-dagger stuff and I wasn't allowed to have any contact with the outside world. Anyone I came into contact with from the show could see I was getting more and more nervous as the programme approached. One of them gave me some advice. 'Just be yourself,' they said.

I knew exactly what they meant, but then thought, 'I don't really know myself!' I'd been Kellie full-time for just a week and now I was about to put myself into the homes of millions of people each night. The thought terrified me.

With about 90 minutes to go until I was due on the show I sat in my dressing room having my make-up done and feeling physically sick. When I was told there were just 15 minutes to go my whole body seemed to break down and I could hear the girl who had been sent to get me urgently talking on her radio.

'I think we've got a problem with KitKat,' she was telling someone.

They asked if I'd like a drink and then within minutes a bottle of wine arrived. I guzzled down a couple of glasses and the show's psychiatrist came to see me. I asked to speak to Jan and to Heather. I was in a real state. I swallowed some more wine and pretty much finished the bottle. The psychiatrist told me he would be with me in the blacked-out car which was to take me to the house. I was being reassured throughout the short journey and by this time I was pretty much on autopilot. This was my final chance to back out. The car stopped and I heard the crowd.

I honestly don't remember walking to the House or speaking to Emma Willis, who was hosting the show, but I obviously did both. The next memory I have is of being in the house and talking to Stephanie Pratt and Audley Harrison. As for the rest of the night I don't really remember any of it. Apparently Lauren Goodger and Dee Kelly found me slumped in the toilet after drinking too much champagne. Not the best of starts for someone who had been warned by Sophie and Libby to behave myself and not do anything silly.

On the first full day I began to feel as though I had made a big mistake. The thing that concerned me most was the fact that I was sharing a living space with so many people. I'd had such a solitary existence for more than a year and suddenly I was living 24 hours a day with 13 other people and, apart from Audley, I didn't know any of them. Lauren, and Stephanie came from the world of reality TV, as did Frenchy Morgan and Ricci Guarnaccio. Dee had become well known for a documentary series called *Benefits Street* and George Gilby was a regular on another reality series called *Goggle-box*. The other people in the house were actress Clare King, singer Edele Lynch, former TV gladiator David McIntosh, American actors Gary Busey and Leslie Jordan, as well as dancer James Jordan.

It was all a bit strange for everyone and I think we were all on our best behaviour to begin with. As part of the negotiations we'd had I was allowed my own bathroom and they weren't allowed to film me in bed in case my wig fell off. It had been explained to the producers of the show that I was still in a pretty vulnerable place and they were very good about the whole thing, including being aware of just how emotional I could become. It didn't really take long for that side of me to come through.

For the first few days I was desperate to get out of the house. Despite Sophie and Libby telling me not to keep crying, I found myself shedding tears on several occasions. I also allowed myself to get wound up by Leslie and Frenchy, which was silly and wrong of me. The trouble was that I was still trying to find Kellie and when the pressure was on, I reverted to the old Frank, even threatening to knock little Leslie spark out! It wasn't my best moment.

I also had a bit of a confrontation with Audley who wasn't comfortable with me being in the big tub with him. I really got upset about this because I saw it as him basically discriminating against me purely because of my transsexuality. There was an awkward atmosphere between us until we had a chat to clear the air. I broke down once again when I was talking to him, but wanted to make Audley understand just how hurtful and horrible it was. I explained that it would be like me saying I wasn't prepared to get in the tub with him because he was black. It would be wrong. I think he began to understand why it had upset me.

'All I've asked for is acceptance,' I told him.

'Man to woman,' Audley replied. 'I apologise.'

We then had a hug and I think we both came away feeling emotionally drained. I understood how difficult it must have been for Audley, he'd known me as Frank for all of his boxing life and he was having trouble coming to terms with that person now being Kellie. I think my approach changed after that talk with Audley. I had a lot of good moments while I was in the house and made some good friends. All the girls were really helpful and we used to chat a lot. George and Ricci were very good to me too, and Audley and I were fine. I used to have a lot of laughs with Dee and Lauren, in particular.

The girls would ask me lots of questions about my transition and what I planned to do. I told them I would probably have my final operation sometime early in 2015. 'So you're going to have your banana split then!' said Dee.

'I've heard it called a lot of things Dee, but never that,' I told her.

I was the fifth person to be voted out after I'd been in the house for two weeks and four days. I came out feeling it had helped me and that feeling grew in the days and weeks which followed. I think I buried Frank when I walked out of the house and I think *Big Brother* was like a finishing school for Kellie. I honestly can't praise the show enough, and I told the producer and staff how much I felt it had helped me. I must have been just about the only transsexual who slowly developed in front of the British public each night.

Perhaps the best thing to come out of it was the fact that Libby and Sophie were able to see Kellie every night. They got used to me. They saw the good, bad and ugly side to me, but I think they also saw the honesty that I always tried to display. I didn't go on the show to bang the drum for transsexuals, but I hope it at least gave the public some sort of insight into what it is like for me and thousands of others like me. I came out knowing just how lucky I was to have the love and support of my family, friends and the public.

While I was in the house my management company received an email from a girl who had written a poem she'd read at her dad's funeral entitled, 'Inner War':

> *My dad's life was a constant war*
> *As I digress you'll understand more.*
> *It wasn't until recently that I found out he had a dream*
> *only he knew about.*
> *I admired my dad and his bravery and strength*
> *But now I know this was his self-defence.*

He'd walk with pride, so manly and tough, what other
people thought he couldn't give a stuff.
Typical man when it came to emotion
But deep within he was brutally broken.
My dad, Robert, wanted to be Robyn
Inside was this woman, for years she'd been sobbing.
As he started to admit who he wanted to be,
My dad he wanted to be a she.
This woman was ready to be true
So I said, 'Dad, I accept you.'
But as he was tortured throughout the years,
Finally admitting it brought painful tears.
He felt alone, trapped and torn
Hence here today is why I mourn.
People would yell, say, 'He's a freak'
As he wore his wig, acceptance he'd seek.
He couldn't handle the pressure or stress
I'm telling him dad you shouldn't care less.
On the phone I'd be
While he cried to me.
'Kayleigh,' he said, 'I just want to be free.
'There is only one way out and I'm sorry.'
People say it's selfish, how my dad died.
To stop him a few times is what I tried.
I won't judge him, what he'd done.
I won't call him selfish, stupid or dumb.
He's at peace now
And to my dad I vow.
I will never forget you
I will always love you.
As you wrote to me in a letter,

*I am your best friend, your princess and above all your
daughter.*
That will never change.

Kayleigh ended her email by saying I was a true inspiration, which
was a lovely of her, but I too had dark thoughts in the past and
tried to take my life. Being transsexual is not easy. It brings with it
all sorts of problems both mental and physical. Sometimes those
problems are just too much to take. Tragically, for many transsexuals, death becomes the only way they feel they can find peace.

CHAPTER TWENTY-TWO

Whole new world

If the reaction of the public to my story being published was amazing, then their reaction to my time in *Celebrity Big Brother* was incredible. I honestly couldn't believe it. A few days after my eviction I had to travel up to London with Emma for a meeting and got stopped so many times by people in the street either wanting to talk or asking to have their picture taken with me.

The other thing I began to notice was that most of the people who recognised me were women, and the nice thing was that they also wanted to stop and have a chat. It was a great feeling for me to know that I seemed to have been accepted by other women. It was also good to find out that despite some of my on-screen meltdowns, the public did seem to genuinely like me and were interested in the whole transgender issue. I think they appreciated how difficult it had been for me to go into the house so soon after publicly coming out as a transsexual.

I was pleased that I'd put transsexualism on the news agenda and that people were now openly talking about it. All I'd ever really wanted as a transsexual was acceptance. I didn't want to be tolerated – that just made it sound like we were a nuisance to society. All I, or any other transsexual, wants to be is part of society. We are not freaks, we are men and women, human beings, but human beings who had the misfortune to be born into the wrong body. I had known all of my life that I should be a woman. I'd fought against it and denied it for so long, but in the end I made the decision to own up to my true feelings and be the person I should be. I wanted to be a woman, and that was what I was going to be. I accepted that I was going to be a medically modified woman, but I was going to be true to myself and I think genetic women could identify with that and understand the torment it must have caused me.

A lot of people had called me brave, but I didn't feel brave. If I was that brave I would have been honest with myself a lot sooner. I was no braver that any other transsexual who is true to themselves. We all have to suffer the consequences of making that decision and so do those who are closest to us. Other transexuals can lose everything because they want to be the person they really know they should be. They are the brave ones. They are the people who suffer and have their lives destroyed. I had those fears as well and I was also worried about public exposure and the effect that would have.

I left *Big Brother* to find my new passport waiting for me. I had filled in all the documentation some time earlier and when I came out there it was. I was officially Kellie and it meant a great deal. A couple of other things happened while I was on the show. I found out that my brother Eugene had given a pretty spiteful interview to a newspaper about me being a transsexual which didn't surprise me. It was sad that he couldn't accept it, but at the same time I wasn't going to lose any sleep over it. Eugene was Eugene.

The more important thing was that some facial feminisation surgery I'd planned for September had to be put back because of me going into the house. It was now going to take place at the beginning of November. Before then I had a couple of trips to Ireland to do TV chat shows. The first was in Dublin and I got to use my new passport for the first time. I flew with my mum and Emma. We had a really nice time and the interview went well. I had to smile to myself when I remembered the trips I'd made there in the past to use the dressing service in secret. It was an indication of just how much my life had changed. Instead of a few snatched hours hidden away dressed as a woman, here I was walking around Dublin as Kellie, shopping with my daughter and mother. At the same time, I had people coming up to me and saying, 'Hello'. The feeling of warmth and acceptance was very special.

So too was the acceptance and warmth I got from a member of my own family a few days later at Emma's house. My nephew, Eugene, who was the son of my brother Eugene, was also staying the night and it was the first time he'd seen Kellie. Unlike his father, young Eugene seemed to take everything in his stride and immediately made me feel at ease. He began calling me Auntie Kellie, which made us all laugh but there was a more serious side to this. Another member of my family had accepted what was going on in my life and given me their support. It meant a lot.

I intended to buy a new house and start living full-time as Kellie in a different location, having spent more than a year living in Maidstone. I felt that a clean break would be best and I liked the idea of living by the coast. I had looked at a few places, but when I came out of the *Big Brother* house, Sophie and Libby had another idea which they thought would be a better solution.

I had owned a flat in Bromley for some time but had rented it out. The flat was about ten minutes away from my old house and the girls suggested that I start living there. It meant they would be near and could pop over regularly. Tracey also thought it was a good idea and the more I thought about it I had to agree with her. It would be great having them all so close and Emma would only be a 30-minute drive away. Having my family nearby and knowing the girls wanted me to be a part of their lives was very special. Emma had been my rock and supported me with everything I'd done for almost two years, but I knew Sophie and Libby were still coming to terms with what had happened and I realised it was difficult for them and for Emma. None of them wanted to lose their dad in the form they had known all of their lives, but all three of them gave me their love, and that was amazing. The thought of losing that love had almost driven me insane in the past, so to have Sophie and Libby being so positive made me feel very special.

The people who had been renting the flat were very understanding and I was able to move in pretty quickly. The place needed decorating and there was a lot of new furniture that I wanted to buy. The girls enjoyed the convenience of me being so close and my nephew Eugene spent a lot of time at the flat in the first few weeks after I moved in, as I used the company he worked for to do all the decorating. Within weeks the place was looking more like the home I wanted.

Having more facial feminisation surgery was not essential, but it was something I wanted to do. Perhaps it was vanity, but I was just trying to make sure I looked like the woman I wanted to be. Having had to postpone the original surgery I was keen to get it done as soon as I could. I'd done quite a lot of research and eventually chose a top surgeon in Antwerp, Belgium. He had an excellent reputation and I felt confident he would be able to do exactly what I wanted. I'd decided that I was going to have the bone in my nose thinned, my cheeks plumped, top and bottom eye lifts and a full facial lift. The surgery I'd had in Spain had gone well and although this was probably a bit more radical, I still felt confident about the end result and the fact that it would help me achieve the look I wanted.

I travelled to Antwerp in my car with the two dogs and Linda on a Sunday, which was a couple of days before the operation was due to take place. Emma was going to meet us the next day at the apartment I'd rented. She arrived too late to go along to the consultation with me 24 hours before the surgery was due to take place, but when I got back from seeing the doctor it was good to see her. I'd come to rely on her for so much and although I was confident that the procedure would go well, I was still nervous about the whole thing.

We were up bright and early on the morning of the surgery and got a taxi to the clinic where I was due to be operated on by the surgeon. He'd explained that he was using the venue because he didn't have his own practice open at the time. When we got there I decided it looked more like a day care centre and it was a bit disconcerting to see my doctor unpacking his car and taking in all the equipment he would need to operate on me later that day. I actually walked into the theatre at about 9.15 am and was later told that everything took about seven hours to complete. Emma wasn't allowed to visit me and the clinic closed at 6.00 pm.

When I eventually came round I was in tremendous pain. I managed to use the phone to call Emma. She told me that she'd tried to call to find out how I was but couldn't get an answer. She said that she'd see me first thing in the morning and that I should get some rest. I tried to do just that, drifting in and out of sleep but by what must have been the early hours of the morning, I was in agony. I was thirsty and wanted some water but got nothing. When Emma arrived in the morning I could tell that she was in shock at what she saw. I was in a lot of pain, but could see the look of horror in her eyes.

I was in a real mess and could feel that there seemed to be blood everywhere. By this time I was not only thirsty, but starving as well. I hadn't eaten anything for about 36 hours and felt absolutely awful. There was one nurse on duty who apparently didn't seem that concerned with the way I was feeling and looking. Emma did her best to try and clean me up, asking for some sterile solution and swabs. Luckily, I couldn't see just how bad I looked, but Emma could, and she has since told me that my face was full of blood. I was even bleeding from the eyes. My surgeon eventually arrived and brought with him a box containing bread, a slice of cheese and a bottle of water. I'd paid a lot of money for the operation and believed I'd got one of the top people in their field. The least I expected was a high level of after-care, but didn't seem to be getting it. He took a look at me and admitted there was more swelling than he would like to see, but thought this could be due to the aspirin that I had been taking until just a few days before the operation. I'd been taking them to thin my blood since my heart attack and had explained all of this during my consultation a couple of days earlier. I was discharged from the clinic, given a bag full of various medication which included painkillers and made my way in the back of a taxi to the apartment with Emma.

I was in a lot of pain and my head felt as if it were going to explode. When I got to the apartment I went to the bathroom and could see for myself how bad I looked. I was unrecognisable. One of my dogs, Winnie, actually ran away from me and began barking. I was this stumbling figure, wandering around the apartment and bleeding all over the floor. I looked more like a Hollywood monster than a human being and the pain seemed to be getting worse by the minute. Emma decided enough was enough. She'd popped out to the shops for some food and when she got back my head had actually got larger. It was like a balloon, getting bigger by the minute and the horrible thing was, I could feel my head expanding. You didn't have to be an expert to realise something was very wrong.

Emma got straight on the phone to the surgeon and he told her he would meet us at a different clinic to the one he'd used for the operation. The taxi journey there was awful. I didn't know what to do with myself. I was still bleeding and spent the entire journey groaning because of the pain I was in. I can't imagine what the taxi driver must have thought, but after what seemed like an eternity, we finally arrived at this place that looked like a brand new hospital. In fact, it was so new that half the equipment was still in its wrapping.

There was quite a long wait before my surgeon was ready to see me and he explained he and his wife, who assisted him, were going to drain blood from my head and hopefully this would solve the problem. It didn't take them long to realise that they wouldn't be able to help and he called a local hospital to say he was sending me along to be treated as a matter of urgency. I was put in a wheelchair and taken down to the car parking area where the doctor's wife was going to use her husband's car to take us to the hospital. When we got to the car we saw that it was a two-seater Porsche! His wife quickly apologised and then said she'd use a people carrier they had. She wheeled me from the car park to a pavement area, while she went to get the people carrier and as I sat there, groaning and dripping blood, a young kid who must have just finished school came running towards me. He suddenly took one look and was so frightened and appalled at what he saw that he virtually burst into tears and swerved out of the way to avoid me.

When we got to the hospital the medical staff could see just how serious the problem was. They acted really quickly and I was looked at both by doctors and by their plastic surgeon. It very soon became clear that this was a real emergency and although I thankfully didn't know it at the time, they realised that my life could be under threat if something wasn't done to stop the bleeding.

Emma could see how bad things were but, like all the staff, she kept trying to reassure me. By this time my blood pressure was racing. There seemed to be a difference of opinion between the doctor who had carried out the facial surgery and the doctors at the hospital as to what procedure they should take. I was asked what I wanted to do and went along with what had been suggested by the hospital, which was to undergo surgery to stop the bleeding. I was aware that the staff at the hospital had been fantastic from the moment I had been wheeled into the place and I had confidence in them.

They quickly began to get me ready for surgery and in the middle of all of this drama there was a light-hearted moment that I didn't really think about at the time because I felt so ill, but which made me smile some time later. The hospital had naturally asked all sorts of questions about me and my health. They had been told that I had been taking hormones and that I was a transsexual. The nurse had to make sure my bladder was empty before they proceeded and got a female bedpan. It wasn't until she took a look under the sheets that she realised I hadn't fully transitioned, so she had to run off and get a male version.

Within two hours of being admitted, I was wheeled off for surgery. Emma gave me a kiss and tried to reassure me once more, but by this time I really knew nothing of what was going on. I was later told that they had to re-open the wounds and pack in gauze to stop the bleeding, leaving the wounds open so that they could gain access quickly if the bleeding continued. If I'd looked like Chucky from the horror movie when I went into the hospital, by the time they brought me out of the operating theatre I resembled an Egyptian mummy. There was very little of my face which wasn't wrapped in bandages, I had a tube coming out of my mouth to help me breathe and another out of the top of my head which helped to drain any blood and fluid. The sight of me was shocking for Emma when she came to see me in intensive care, but she was reassured by the doctors.

I was kept sedated and hooked up to a machine which helped me to breathe. They decided that the operation had been a success so they sewed up the wounds and began the process of bringing me round. It had been a couple of days since I'd undergone surgery and I felt very low when I regained consciousness. Emma tried to tell me that my face hadn't been mucked up by what had gone on.

My nephew Eugene travelled out to be with Emma and give her some support, which was really good of him. Rich also came out a day later and took my car home with Linda and the dogs. By the time I was allowed to leave hospital it was a week after the original surgery. Emma and Eugene travelled back to England with me by train a few days later.

I recuperated with Emma and I vowed that I would never have cosmetic surgery again. Perhaps I'd paid a heavy price for being too vain? One thing was for sure. What I'd done had affected Emma and the rest of my family. There were some bad moments after I got back to England when I wondered what the hell I would end up looking like but after seeing a facial surgeon in Brighton, I was assured that things would eventually be okay. I needed to let everything settle down and allow nature to take its course with the healing process.

I gradually began to get back to normal and early in December I went for a consultation at the hospital in Brighton where I was due to have the operation that would see me fully transition. They seemed to think that the surgery could take place in March 2015. Finally, I was going to be a woman. The realisation that I was now in touching distance of being the person I always should have been was not only an exciting moment but a very emotional one as well.

I was really looking forward to the Christmas and New Year period. It would be my last with my family before I fully transitioned. Just before the holidays I took a trip to New York with Libby for a few days and we had a lovely time. We did quite a bit of shopping and it was great to spend time with her. She was still only 13 years old and the thought of the night I told her about myself, just over a year earlier, still made me shudder. Just like Emma and Sophie, she'd had a lot to take on board, but I thought she'd managed to cope well with it. There had been some difficult moments, but I was in a very different place now to the one I'd been in when I locked Libby and her mother in the bedroom. Although she was young she often surprised me with her maturity. She'd come along with me to my support group meetings and joined in and was clearly keen to try and understand more of what it was like for people like her dad and also for their children and families.

I might not have shown it all the time, but I was very conscious of the fact this was still very early days for all of my daughters.

They might have put brave faces on for me, but I knew they had their private moments where they must have wondered what the hell had happened to their lives. The great thing was the effort, support and love they showed me. I honestly don't know what I would have done without Emma at my side. I'm sure she thought I took her for granted at times, but that was never the case. Sophie and Libby would pop in and make themselves at home whenever they wanted to and it made me really happy to see the way they now felt more comfortable with me as Kellie. It was funny and really nice hearing Sophie ask me if she could borrow my make-up or a pair of tights. I was so grateful for it.

The contrast between Christmas 2013 and Christmas 2014 was amazing. Twelve months earlier I only had my two lovely dogs for company, this time I was surrounded by people and loved it. On Christmas Eve Sophie and Libby came over and stayed. On Christmas morning we opened our presents and cards including one I'd got from my mum which read, 'To a very special daughter.' There were a few tears from me but they were tears of happiness and I then went off to have lunch with Emma and Rich.

On Boxing Day we'd all been invited over to my nephew Eugene's house for a real old-style Christmas party. I loved every minute of it and everyone there was so nice to me. All of his friends were tremendous and I never once felt anything other than total acceptance. On New Year's Eve I went for a meal with some girlfriends and Sophie turned up. She was having a night out with friends in a bar across the road. We went over to join them and I ended the night by kicking off my high heels and walking home quite drunk, having relaxed a little bit too much with the help of a few bottles of pink champagne.

When I woke up the next morning with a sore head it was as if Frank had been in the flat the night before. As Kellie I had always been very precise about looking after my clothes when I took them off. I would hang them up and make sure I put them away in my wardrobe, but as I looked around the bedroom and the rest of the flat I saw a trail of clothes scattered on the floor. It was just the sort of thing I used to do as Frank when I came in from a night out. I met Emma and Rich for lunch on New Year's Day and then saw them again the next evening for a dinner, I was feeling quite nervous about.

It was at this meal that I would be meeting my great friend Tommy Pratt for the first time as Kellie. Since being told about me by Emma five months earlier, Tommy had sent me some really nice messages and had made it clear from the moment he knew I was transsexual that he was still my friend. Tommy and his wife, Donna, could not have been nicer and it wasn't long before we were all laughing and joking just as we always had done. Tommy did call me Frank quite a bit, which I had no problem with at all. I'm not the sort of person who is going to get precious or upset about something like that. How can I suddenly expect people who have known me for so long as Frank to instantly switch? Of course it's strange for them to start calling me Kellie, but it's their friendship which I value most. Tommy had been a good friend in the past and I knew, having now met him as Kellie, that he would continue to be my friend in the future and that meant a lot to me.

One person I was not looking forward to meeting as Kellie was a guy called Jamie. He was someone I'd known in Portugal for quite a few years. He was a native of the Algarve, a bit older than me and a real man's man. Jamie often came up to the house to do various jobs for me, got on really well with my dad and the two of them used to go out drinking together. I also used to pay for Jamie to come over and go to some of the fights I promoted.

He loved boxing and I knew he also thought of me as this tough little macho guy.

I went to Portugal to celebrate my birthday in January with Eugene and my two dogs. My nephew was going to be doing some work on the house for me. Tracey had told me that quite a few people we knew in Portugal had read all about me in the newspapers. I suspected Jamie knew too, but I hadn't seen him since the previous summer so I decided to drive over to his house and speak to him. When I arrived and knocked on his door there was no answer, so I left him a note on a piece of paper written with my lipstick saying that I was staying at my house. I waited to see if he would turn up that evening but it wasn't until the next day that we met. He got out of his car, asking a question as he did. 'And how is Miss Kellie Maloney?' he said, with a smile.

'I'm very good, Jamie,' I replied.

'Are you happy?' he asked.

'Yes, Jamie,' I told him, 'Very happy.'

He walked towards me and gave me a cuddle. It was a lovely moment and made me feel so relieved. We went inside the house and chatted for ages just as we always had done. It was as if nothing had changed.

It seemed as though my life was beginning to look so much more positive than it had done for years. I was still getting a lot of goodwill from the public and there also seemed to be continued interest from the media, which was something I hadn't really expected. I was determined to enjoy my birthday and I did. Emma and Rich paid me a surprise visit and I also had a couple of other friends out with me. It just felt so different to be able to do things like this without worrying. I was able to do all the normal things I'd hoped to do and I knew that having my final operation two months later meant 2015 would be a special year.

I had already ticked a lot of boxes when it came to things I wanted to do now that I was Kellie, but there was still something outstanding. Millwall had played a big part in my life since I was a kid. I'd always loved going to watch them even though it could often be frustrating. They weren't a big club, they weren't fashionable and they weren't particularly successful. But they were my club and they always would be. I'd been invited by Mark Cole, their commercial sales manager, to talk at one of their business breakfast meetings early in February. It went well and I was pleased to be back at the club. The people I gave the talk to were really nice to me and I got a good reception, but as I talked to them I wondered what the reception might be like for me a few days later when I planned to return as a fan to watch the team's match against Huddersfield. It was something which made me really nervous whenever I thought about it, but like so many of the other concerns I'd had about what it would be like when I was finally Kellie, I need not have worried.

I was able to use my friend Tony Fry's box at the ground and invited along quite a few old friends, including Ray Hawkins, who had yet to meet Kellie. I knew it had been hard for him to come to terms with me, but like Tommy, his friendship meant a lot and when he turned up at Millwall that day it was fantastic to see him. It didn't take long before he was joking about some of the things the two of us had got up to in the past. It was as if nothing had changed and what came through was his friendship and that of everyone who came along on the day. One thing which definitely hadn't changed was the disappointment my beloved team were capable of causing for their long-suffering fans. Millwall lost 3–1.

I had been looking forward to my final operations for so long, but as the time approached I suddenly began to feel anxious. I suppose it was a combination of things. It was obviously a major moment in my life and this was going to be the final piece in the jigsaw, but having gone through the trauma of what had happened in Belgium there was also a bit of fear. I knew it was only natural and I also knew I had complete faith in the medical people who were going to be doing the surgery.

I was due to have my surgery on at the Nuffield hospital in Brighton on Tuesday 24 March. It was to be a double operation and I'd be having my breast implants done and also my full vaginoplasty. I tried to do as much as I could to take my mind off of what was going to happen but it was difficult. The memory of what had happened in Belgium was still very vivid and I knew that was also the case for Emma. Neither of us really wanted to talk about that terrible time and when she came to pick me up to take me down to Brighton, I think we both felt nervous and awkward. We tried to make small talk and keep everything upbeat but it was tough. I'd waited and dreamed of the moment I would have the surgery to put right what had been wrong at birth. This was permanent, it was what I wanted, I was going to feel complete, but I knew it was going to be very emotional for Emma and the rest of my family.

Emma helped me settle into my room and could see how edgy I was. She did her best to calm me down, but when they checked me over it was clear my blood pressure was high and if it had not come down they would have called the whole thing off. Emma stayed with me until the evening before leaving me to try and get some sleep, but when she'd gone I felt quite restless and my mind was racing. After years of mental turmoil I would finally put things right and find the inner peace I'd wanted since those days as a kid when I'd dreamed I was a little girl and not a little boy. For years I had denied what I really was and tried to conform to what was expected of me. I had lied, covered up my true feelings and built an image that even those closest to me did not know was false. I had terrible regrets about not owning up to myself and others earlier in my life, but after all the torment I had eventually been driven to do something, to take control and to finally be me. I knew I had caused heartache, pain and suffering to those closest to me. I hoped they would forgive me and understand that ultimately I had no real control over what had driven me towards this final piece in the jigsaw of my transition from man to woman.

On the morning of the operation the nurses were in and out of my room from about 6.00 am, getting me ready for the two operations I was going to have. Emma arrived at around seven to sit with me while I waited to be wheeled down to the theatre. I was going to have the breast procedure first and the operation was done by Mr Andrew Yelland. I'd had consultations with him about the size and shape that would suit me and the kind of lifestyle I had. He had been very precise and reassuring about how I would look and feel once he had operated on me and I was confident I would be pleased with the end result.

My vaginoplasty operation was carried out by Mr Phil Thomas and it was going to give me a working vagina, as opposed to a cosmetic one which was an alternative. I would later have to learn about douching and dilating, something that was going to be part of my life for ever. Duncan Macdonald was the anaesthetist and he was very reassuring. Knowing that my blood pressure had been high the day before, he explained that he would be monitoring me throughout.

Just before I was due to go to the operating theatre, Liz Hills, the gender nurse, came in to have a chat. She was lovely and could tell Emma and I were both really nervous. Liz told me that I could pull back from having the procedure at any time if I wasn't completely sure it was what I wanted, but there was no doubt in my mind.

Just as I was about to be wheeled down Emma gave me a kiss and told me that she would see me when they brought me back. They took me down and I waited patiently to be wheeled into the actual operating theatre. The two operations were scheduled to take around five hours but after what seemed like seconds I remember being back in my room and being told the operations had been a complete success. I drifted in and out of consciousness and stared up at Emma's face as I lay there on my back. I told her how much I loved her and asked if it felt like she'd lost her dad. She told me not to be silly, but I knew it must be tough for her and for Sophie and Libby too.

One of the things I had been worried and depressed about on countless occasions throughout my journey towards fully transitioning was the effect it would have on my family and the relationship I'd have with my three daughters. It was difficult for all of them when they found out about their dad, but one by one as each of them had been told, they somehow found a way to cope and try to come to terms with what was an enormous change to their lives. Their love and support had been so important to me. No father wants to lose the love of their children. My transition had not been easy for me. There were huge ups and downs along the way, but I realised it had not been easy for all of my family and in particular for my mother, Tracey, Emma, Sophie and Libby.

When Libby and I had taken that holiday in New York we were questioned at passport control when we arrived back in the UK. The surname in my new passport was not Maloney – I'd decided on a different name some time earlier but everyone calls me Kellie Maloney. The passport official saw that Libby and I had different surnames and asked what our relationship was.

'I'm her dad,' I told the surprised official.

'Yes,' said Libby with a cheeky smile on her face. 'She's my dad!'

It was lovely to hear her say it. As far as she was concerned I was still the same person and still her dad. All I was really doing was changing the wrapping.